Library of Congress Cataloging-in-Publication Data

Kelly, William J., 1953-
  Home safe home: how to make your home environmentally safe by William J. Kelly.
  256 p. 15 x 23 cm.
  "A Plain English Press book."
  Bibliography: p.
  Includes index.
  ISBN 0-915765-70-5: $9.95
  1. Indoor air pollution. 2. Housing and health.   I. Title
RA577.5.K45 1989
613'.5--dc20
                                    89-12538
                                        CIP

PRINTED IN THE UNITED STATES OF AMERICA
First Edition

How to Make Your Home Environmentally Safe

Plain
English
Press

National
Press
Books

Table of Contents

Table Contents

Chapter One

Environmental Hazards

in the Home

The house, my first, stood on a quiet tree-lined street in the suburbs of Washington, D.C. It was a tranquil retreat, a quarter of a green acre tucked away from the car exhaust, noise, malodorous sewers, and grime I faced downtown in the nation's capital where I covered environmental affairs as a reporter. It seemed so far away from my daily preoccupation with stories on toxic pollutants, acid rain, sewage and contaminated drinking water.

But the stories I covered began to shift from outdoor pollution to indoor pollution as concern emerged over radon, lead in household plumbing, asbestos, pesticides at home, indoor air pollution, and the list goes on. Indeed, environmental scientists were warning that the home is where you are most likely to be exposed to toxic chemicals. Heeding their warning, I began to look around my own.

In the gutters beneath the fall leaves I found particles from weathered and disintegrating asbestos roof shingles. In my basement, I found mold covering the underside of the carpet. Moreover, the smell of mold permeated the house when the central air conditioner ran. When I needed to rid my front porch of a wasp infestation, an exterminator came and pumped insecticides for ten minutes straight into my bedroom wall. I could smell the chemicals for more than a month. Then when I opened the windows on temperate nights after the leaves had fallen, I could hear the roar of a nearby freeway. I looked at the copper water pipes, which appeared to be welded with lead solder. And I always wondered, but was scared to inquire about radon.

How did I get into this? As an environmental reporter I knew that businesses were well aware of such environmental hazards and made closing commercial real estate deals contingent upon identifying and solving contamination problems in buildings and on the grounds. Yet, individuals rarely do the same in their own homes or in residential real estate sales. And by not doing so many are buying ill health.

Environmental authorities are beginning to grapple with the problem of household pollution. For instance, the Massachusetts Legislature recently enacted a law to make inspection of homes for lead contamination standard before they are sold. Yet lead is just one potential problem and Massachusetts but one state.

The new revelations of toxic hazards in the home come after some two decades of government action to control pollution outdoors. When public outrage over pollution culminated in the Earth Day demonstration, Congress in the early 1970's responded by passing landmark environmental laws. Since then, the Environmental Protection Agency has enforced these laws to cut back on pollution from autos, city sewers and industry. Almost 20 years later, the air and waterways are noticeably cleaner. Yet, environmental officials have found themselves asking how much better protected the public really is from toxic hazards. The reason? More sophisticated ways of detecting toxics have shown that some of the most significant exposures occur where you spend most of your time, namely at home. Environmental scientists now believe that for all these years you probably have inhaled and ingested more toxics in the comfort of your own home and other buildings than in the air outside and the waterways.

The dangers of indoor toxic hazards were clearly demonstrated in EPA's recent "Total Exposure Assessment Methodology Studies." These studies showed that people living in rural areas and cities with light industry suffer the same exposure to toxics as people in heavily industrialized areas. You are just as likely to suffer exposure to toxics in rural North Dakota as in smog-clouded Los Angeles or the chemical industry center of Elizabeth, N.J. This is because, the most significant toxic hazards occur in the course of everyday activities, many of which take place in the home.

While this conclusion may seem hard to believe, consider that houses are full of toxic materials.

Asbestos

Asbestos insulation, roofing shingles and other construction materials were used widely in homebuilding for many years. When the fibers enter the air as the materials deteriorate their inhalation can cause a fatal, cancer-like disease of the lungs. Many uses of asbestos have been banned by EPA and the Consumer Product Safety Commission. But, according to EPA, homes built between World War II and the 1960's frequently have asbestos in them. Congress has ordered that asbestos be removed from schools. Efforts are under way to remove it from most public buildings. However, it will be up to individuals to discover if they have asbestos in their homes and to have it removed or encapsulated.

Pesticides

About 30 million homes have been treated, often mistreated, with the banned pesticides chlordane and heptachlor, which have been implicated as carcinogens in laboratory tests. The manufacturer of the pesticides recently agreed with EPA not to sell them for use in the home until perfecting ways to safely apply them. However, these two products are not the only ones that have been frequently used and misused in the home to kill insects and other pests. Based on a nationwide survey of pesticide use, EPA estimates that extermination companies have treated 16.7 million homes for pests other than termites. In the case of chlordane and heptachlor, it was misapplication by such commercial services that led the maker to take the products off the market. Surely many of the other pesticides used in the home have been misapplied. In fact, EPA found widespread problems in its National Household Pesticide Usage Study. More than 500 pesticides are used in homes. Nine out of 10 homes have had pesticides used in or around them. And two percent of those surveyed reported mishaps with pesticides in the home.

Radon Contamination

EPA estimates up to 20,000 cases of lung cancer occur each year due to household exposure to radioactive radon gas. While the problem was first highlighted in 1984 along the Reading Prong, a geological formation stretching through Pennsylvania, New Jersey, and New York, a survey since conducted by EPA shows high household levels of radon across the country. Environmental authorities are continuing to pinpoint areas where radon presents a danger.

Lead in Children

Lead poisoning continues to be a problem, even after levels of lead in gasoline have been drastically reduced and most cars now run on unleaded gasoline. EPA estimates more than 42 million Americans may be exposed to excessive levels through lead used in their household water pipes. This is particularly tragic for children. Lead poisoning in children causes lifelong learning disabilities and stunted physical growth. To help solve the problem of lead in drinking water, Congress in 1986 banned use of lead pipes and lead solder to connect water pipes. The ban will prevent future problems, but will not address existing ones. That will be up to individual homeowners.

Lead in the soil surrounding a house can be a problem. Lead paint chips, broken up and accumulated in yards as homes are repainted, have been implicated as a cause of lead poisoning in children who play in and often ingest dirt. Where your home is located also can play a role in how much lead is in the yard. Homes near heavily traveled highways or streets have high accumulations of lead in the soil, the fallout of years, even decades of exhaust from cars burning leaded gasoline. Concerned over lead in soil, EPA has given Superfund money to three cities to study how contamination in residential neighborhoods can be cleaned up.

Polluted Well-water

Despite publicity about trace contamination of big city water systems, the number one problem with drinking water occurs for those who live in homes served by private wells. In rural areas, wells often are contaminated with nitrates from farming fertilizer, which when ingested in sufficient quantities can make it hard for the blood to carry oxygen. Pesticide contamination also is a common problem. These contaminants can leach down through the soil into the water table. Another common problem is that wells are not adquately sealed, which can allow materials spilled near them on the surface to run down into the well hole. Septic tanks pollute groundwater too. Household chemicals, cleansers, paints, and solvents dumped down the drain can wind up in well water.

Bad Neighbors

It is frightfully common for housing developments to be built on land once used to dump hazardous waste, either in municipal landfills before the practice was banned, or in dumps in old industrial areas that have been turned into bedroom communities for the growing population of office workers and their families. The problem was first and perhaps most dramatically discovered at Love Canal in New York state, where industrial wastes seeped into basements in a neighborhood and 500 homes had to be evacuated permanently. EPA estimates there are more than 20,000 abandoned hazardous waste sites in the United States. Many are in residential areas. In one recent cleanup, a mobile home park in Arizona was evacuated and demolished after high levels of asbestos were discovered. It had been built atop an old asbestos mine.

And what about dangers posed by nearby industrial facilities or warehouses? Concern over a seeming rash of toxic clouds released from such facilities caused Congress in 1986 to include a new title in the Superfund amendments, known as the Emergency Planning and Community-Right-to-Know Act. It requires for the first time that firms publicly disclose what chemicals they are using in neighborhoods across the land.

Toxic Chemicals at Home

EPA has also found that some of the most significant exposures to toxics are attibutable to gases given of by products commonly used in home construction and furnishings. Formaldehyde from pressed wood and vinyl chloride from synthetic materials are among the common ones. Pesticides and other chemicals stored at home produce low levels of toxics as well. The American Lung Association estimates that such indoor air pollution, exclusive of radon, causes up to 16,000 cases of lung cancer a year.

Ventilation

Inadequate ventilation of gas stoves, furnaces, dryers, and water heaters can cause buildup of **carbon monoxide** and nitrogen dioxide in the home. Low levels of these gases, like smog outside, can sap personal energy and irritate the eyes and respiratory tract.

There are a multitude of other environmental dangers at home. For instance, there are underground tanks for storing fuel oil, and sometimes gasoline, in millions of country homes. These can rust out and leak into groundwater. If you own or are buying a country home, beware of this because it probably has a private well.

Alarmed by the potential dangers of pollution in the home, Congress is again contemplating action. Lawmakers are considering setting up an indoor air pollution office at EPA and are moving to establish a new law on radon. Other legislation may be in the offing.

But until Congress acts, environmental officials can take only limited steps. For the most part, it is up to you to protect yourself and your family against exposure to toxics in the home. You must educate yourself, have the proper tests conducted, and when there is a problem, take remedial steps. Also, as a consumer, it is necessary to properly handle chemicals and materials that contain toxics in your home to avoid unnecessary exposures.

Other Health Hazards at Home

Finally, not all dangers involve toxics. In California and other areas earthquakes pose a substantial danger. You must make sure your house is structurally sound and be prepared to ride out the aftermath should the "big one" occur. Noise pollution is another troubling environmental factor. It has been documented to cause stress and fatigue at high decibel levels.

And noise, toxics, and other environmental problems in the home are by no means confined by national boundaries, although the examples here are from the United States. Canada and the northern European countries, with their cold climates and tight seals on homes, suffer from indoor air pollution. In Canada and throughout the industrialized world, for instance, toxic chemicals are used by businesses and industries that border residential neighborhoods.

Fortunately, what you need to know to protect yourself is relatively simple and will entail only minor lifestyle changes in most cases. Solving household environmental problems usually is not expensive. Moreover, while the odds are that you or your family never will suffer from chemically-related illnesses due to exposure at home or experience a devastating earthquake, as the old saying goes, "An ounce of prevention is worth a pound of cure."

So here is a brief description of the types of environmental problems found in the home, their causes, health risks, remedies, and where to turn for help. Armed with this knowledge, you will be an effective negotiator with the home seller on environmental problems and will know how to select an environmental monitoring firm and a contractor to perform needed work. And whether you are just buying or already a proud owner, you'll know how to insure a healthy home environment for your family.

Chapter Two

Indoor Air Pollution

One chilly November night in Los Angeles, Lillian Decatu awoke at 4 a.m. feeling faint and nauseous. She stood up and momentarily fainted before struggling to the bathroom to vomit. From there she hobbled to the front door and opened it for fresh air. Her husband and children laid sick, so Decatu crawled to the phone and dialed 911.

When paramedics arrived, they found Decatu's husband and seven children suffering from the same symptoms. The family's night of sickness, reported in the *Herald Examiner*, followed several days of headaches and times when the children mysteriously fell down. Upon reflection, Decatu realized their troubles began after she turned on the gas furnace for the cold season. In the hospital, doctors diagnosed the family as suffering from carbon monoxide poisoning. Inspectors found that the furnace vent was blocked, causing carbon monoxide produced by the flame to build up in the home. In short, Decatu and family could have died from the deadly, but odorless and invisible carbon monoxide gas had she not acted in time.

Carbon monoxide is one of the most problemmatical outdoor pollutants, since it is produced in great quantities by automobiles. But it is also produced at lower levels in furnaces and other fuel-burning appliances in the home.

While Decatu's story is an extreme instance of carbon monoxide poisoning, it highlights the ultimate danger of indoor air pollution. Luckily, pollutants do not often build up to levels that cause acute poisoning. But envir-

AIR POLLUTION SOURCES IN THE HOME

1. Moisture
2. Pressed Wood Furniture
3. Humidifier
4. Moth Repellents
5. Dry Cleaned Goods
6. House Dust Mites
7. Personal Care Products
8. Air Freshener
9. Stored Fuels
10. Car Exhaust
11. Paint Supplies
12. Paneling
13. Wood Stove
14. Tobacco Smoke
15. Carpets
16. Pressed Wood Subflooring
17. Drapes
18. Fireplace
19. Household Chemicals
20. Asbestos Floor Tiles
21. Pressed Wood Cabinets
22. Unvented Gas Stove
23. Asbestos Pipe Wrap
24. Radon
25. Unvented Clothes Dryer
26. Pesticides
27. Stored Hobby Products

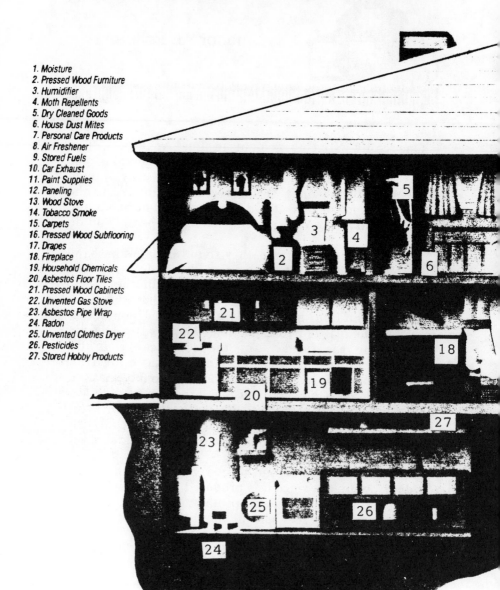

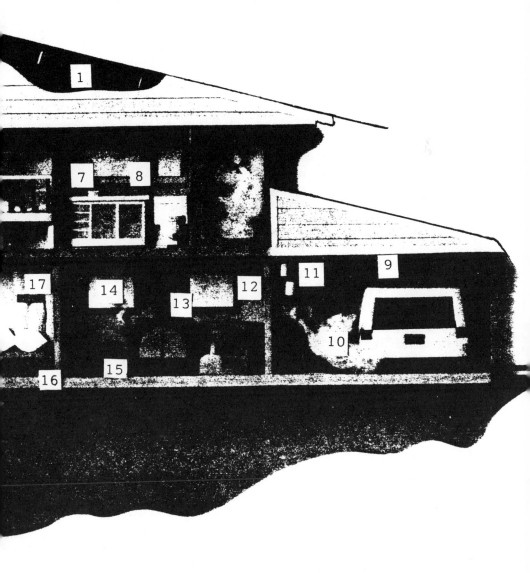

onmental scientists have learned that carbon monoxide and other pollutants present dangers at lower levels, anything from nagging irritation to life threatening diseases.

In fact, after twenty years of reducing outdoor air pollution from automotive tailpipes and industrial smokestacks, the Environmental Protection Agency has concluded that indoor air pollution poses a greater health threat. Studies conducted by EPA in the mid-1980's show little difference in exposure to toxic air pollutants between inhabitants of rural areas with few cars and industries and urban dwellers who live near major oil refineries and chemical plants. The reason? Most people spend 90 percent of their time indoors and about 50 percent in their homes. "Indoor exposures to ... toxic and carcinogenic chemicals," EPA says, "are nearly always greater—much greater—than outdoor concentrations." Concentrations range anywhere from five to 100 times higher, depending upon the pollutant.

Here are the findings, in either parts per million (ppm) or parts per billion (ppb) of some studies comparing pollutant levels indoors and outdoors:

Pollutant	Indoors	Outdoor
Formaldehyde	1.2-3.3 ppm	0.6-1.9 ppm
Carbon Monoxide	150 ppb	4.3-33.3 ppb
Chloroform	43 ppb	26.7 ppb
Carbon Tetrachloride	170 ppb	79 ppb
Benzene	160 ppb	28 ppb
Perchloroethylene	37 ppb	4 ppb
1,1,1-Trichloroethane	1.5 ppm	0.001 ppm
Nitrogen Dioxide	30-32.5 ppb	5-7.5 ppb

Environmental scientists first recognized indoor air pollution as a problem during the energy crisis of the 1970's when homeowners and builders rushed to conserve on heating and cooling. Urea-formaldehyde foam insulation was identified as a key culprit in a rash of developing health problems. Insulation contractors used the foam widely because it could be injected in liquid form into walls where it hardened in place. Walls did not have to be ripped open and put back together as with glass insulation.

But occupants of these newly insulated homes suffered from acute eye, nose, and respiratory tract irritation. After several studies, environmental scientists attributed these ailments to the foam insulation's slow release of formaldehyde. And once released, the formaldehyde tended to reach critical levels because it was trapped by the tightly sealed windows, doors, and walls used to conserve energy by cutting down on air flow. Further studies revealed that formaldehyde was used to make plywood and particle board, materials commonly found in homes and furniture. High levels of formaldehyde were particularly prevalent in mobile homes, which contain large quantities of these materials.

In response, the Consumer Product Safety Commission in 1982 banned the sale of urea-formaldehyde foam insulation. Although a federal court overturned the ban in response to a suit filed by the insulation industry, the negative publicity that stemmed from the commission's action generally killed the product's market. The commission also has been working with wood product manufacturers to minimize use of formaldehyde.

In retrospect, the actions on formaldehyde were just the opening salvo in what promises to be a long war against indoor air pollution. In the late 1980's, the Environmental Protection Agency warns that formaldehyde, now considered a cause of sinus and other forms of cancer, is just one indoor air pollutant. Asbestos, radon, and pesticides pose major risks in household air, as do many other pollutants. EPA says the major classes of indoor air pollutants that may lurk in your home are:

• **Combustion byproducts**, such as **carbon monoxide**, from tobacco, furnaces, stoves, water heaters and other appliances;

• Pollutants released from **construction materials** and

furnishings, such as **formaldehyde;**

• **Biological contaminants** that thrive in moist areas, including air conditioning systems;

• **Fumes** people introduce by using moth balls, cleansers, paints, pesticides and other household chemical products; and

• **Outside contaminants** that enter the home, such as industrial and automotive air pollutants and radon.

The list of individual indoor air pollutants is long and the level of each varies based on a home's individual circumstances. Moreover, the health effects of the pollutants vary, as do the techniques for reducing their concentrations, which can be as simple as keeping your windows slightly ajar, to as complicated and expensive as installing heat exchangers and other equipment.

Health Effects of Indoor Pollutants

Although environmental researchers have assembled much evidence, the health effects of indoor air pollutants, with some exceptions, are generally not well understood. This lack of medical knowledge was underscored by a bill introduced in the 100th Congress that would have required EPA to develop "health advisories" establishing a safe level for each indoor pollutant. Sen. George Mitchell (D-Maine), author of the bill, said data on safe levels are essential for "parties to identify and respond to contamination cases."

One key reason scientists do not fully understand the health effects of indoor air pollution is that the pollutants are so numerous. In one recent study, EPA identified more than 500 types of volatile organic compounds in indoor air. The compounds, nicknamed VOC's, are derived from petroleum and used in a wide variety of building materials, furnishings, and household products.

In addition to VOC's, many other chemicals are found

in indoor air, such as nitrogen dioxide and carbon monoxide. Scientists have studied these two pollutants enough to set health standards for exposure in outdoor air, since they are common components of smog.

But relatively few pollutants are understood individually and even less is known about the health effects of combinations of pollutants found in homes. (The accompanying table summarizes what is known about indoor air pollutants.)

While much is uncertain, EPA has concluded that the wide array of indoor pollutants causes a fair proportion of the eye, nose and throat irritation, headaches, dizziness and fatigue suffered by millions of Americans each day. Further, EPA says, indoor air pollution reduces your resistance to sickness and can specifically cause asthma, hypersensitivity pneumonitis, and other chronic ailments.

Each person's reaction and sensitivity varies. Some may not experience symptoms at all until being sensitized, a phenomenon in which the immune system is conditioned to react after repeated exposure to pollutants. Once sensitized, you may have as minor a reaction as a runny nose or one as serious as asthma. If your symptoms occur at home, but clear up after being away for several hours or days, you have a potential indoor air pollution problem. If you have a history of respiratory disease or allergies, you are more likely to be immediately affected by indoor air pollution. Twenty-five million Americans suffer from chronic respiratory illnesses, 10 percent of the population, according to the Department of Health and Human Service's Center for Health Statistics.

Beyond irritation and allergic respiratory ailments, EPA warns that prolonged exposure to some indoor air pollutants can cause emphysema, heart disease, and cancer. Radon, asbestos, pesticides (covered in separate chapters) and formaldehyde are well documented killers.

Formaldehyde, the National Center for Toxicological Research says, normally occurs at levels below .05 parts per million in outdoor urban air, where it is produced by automobilies. You can smell formaldehyde at .05 ppm and it irritates your eyes at .10 ppm, a level commonly found in new mobile homes. At 1.0 ppm, the federal workplace standard, formaldehyde irritates your nose and throat. Finally, at at 5.0 ppm, the peak level found in homes with urea-formaldehyde insulation, the chemical irritates your lower air passages and lungs. Studies cited by the center also indicate mobile home residents who breathe air containing .10 ppm of formaldehyde increase their chance of contracting cancer by up to one in 5,000 over a lifetime of exposure. To put this in perspective, a cancer risk of one in 5,000 is about twice as high as the risk of cancer and death from heavy drinking.

Less is known about the potential of most pollutants to cause cancer and other fatal diseases. But as indoor air pollution is further studied, it is likely environmental and public health authorities will find other pollutants that lead to fatal diseases. In the interim, home owners and buyers should perform a basic check for indoor air pollution problems.

Inspecting for Indoor Pollutants

It is virtually impossible to screen a home for every indoor air pollutant, since there are so many. Yet to protect yourself and family before buying a home it is imperative to inspect for potential sources of trouble, such as cancer-causing asbestos, and to have air samples tested for radon and chlordane. You also should strongly consider measuring levels of carbon monoxide, carbon dioxide, and formaldehyde. If you already own a home and you or any family member suffers from periodic respiratory irritation you should inspect and screen for these pollutants. And whether you own a home or not, you owe it to yourself to check for radon.

Radon is a naturally occuring radioactive gas that enters homes through cracks and crevices from the ground (see Chapter Three). Chlordane is a pesticide that was used to kill termites until being withdrawn from the market due to health concerns (see Chapter Six). Asbestos is a fibrous material used widely through much of this century in insultation and other building materials on account of its fire retardant qualities (see Chapter Four).

In a 1988 policy responding to growing concern over "sick office building syndrome," the General Services Administration decided that carbon monoxide, carbon dioxide, and formaldehyde are good indicators of overall indoor air quality. GSA, which manages the buildings where more than 2 million federal employees work, set levels for these three pollutants that, when exceeded, indicate an indoor air pollution problem. Although the standards are intended for office buildings, they are among the only federal indoor air quality standards to date and can be readily transferred to the home. GSA's policy is "to protect workers and public visitors so that they are not exposed to unnecessary health risks in federal buildings."

The standards for offices are based upon levels deemed acceptable by other agencies and professional organizations. They are as follows:

Pollutant	Indicator Level	Pollutant Source
Carbon Monoxide	9 ppm	smoking and fuel combustion
Carbon Dioxide	1,000 ppm	human respiration, fuel combustion, smoking
Formaldehyde	0.1 ppm	fumes from building materials and furnishings

GSA's general policy is to assess all buildings for indoor air quality before federal occupancy and renovated buildings before reoccupancy. In addition, GSA pledges to assess indoor air quality in response to complaints. The assessment is to include measurements for the indicator pollutants and a visual inspection for such things as:

- **Direct venting** of furnaces, stoves and water heaters;

- **Damp areas** where mold and bacteria may fluorish;

- Possible **asbestos-containing materials;** and

- Proper overall **ventilation.**

Also, vents should not be located next to potential sources of outdoor air pollution, such as parking garages, loading docks where trucks idle, or gasoline stations. While this is generally not the case in residential areas, in urban settings many residences are in areas where mixed land use is the rule rather than the exception. Finally, use your nose to detect any suspicious odors, including sewer gas, mold from air conditioning ducts, or pungent chemicals.

Here are some additional visual inspection tips:

- Check the furnace to see if the flame is yellow-tipped, which indicates improper adjustment or some other defect. Yellow-tipped flames mean the furnace is burning fuel inefficiently, thereby producing more pollutants.

- Check fireplace chimneys and flues for any blockages, leaks, or damage.

- Ask if the home has urea-formaldehye foam insulation. If it does, make sure it is not damp and that there are no cracks in the walls. Generally, formaldehyde emissions from the foam decline with time. The foam has not been used since the 1970's, so it generally will not still emit high levels of formaldehyde unless wet or exposed.

- Make sure the foundation is sealed, since air entering a home from the soil can contain more moisture than all activities in the home generate. This will help prevent mold. Moreover, pesticides sprayed to kill termites under a home and radon enter through cracks and gaps in the foundation.

EPA is more reluctant to recommend testing of buildings and homes for indoor air pollution problems, except for radon. "For pollutants other than radon, measurements are most appropriate when there are either health symptoms or signs of poor air flow and specific sources of pollutants have been identified as possible causes of indoor air quality problems," EPA advises home owners. Testing for the many potential pollutants can be expensive, so it is wise to consult with state or local health departments (see Appendix for a list) or indoor air professionals before retaining a testing firm.

Regulatory agencies are coping with a large number of indoor air pollutants, of which the health risks are generally little known. Therefore, they are reluctant to recommend that the general public engage in wholesale testing.

When the health risks are well understood and are quite high, as with asbestos and radon, EPA has not been reluctant to recommend testing. The agency recommends checks for both these pollutants and has gone as far as certifying testing firms and contractors.

EPA's approach may be sound for the homeowner, but as a homebuyer you have no way of knowing whether you are purchasing trouble without an inspection and some testing. GSA is concerned enough about federal workers to test all new building space for the indicator pollutants. You should be concerned too, but also aware of some key differences between office buildings and homes.

Modern office workers cannot open their windows. Buildings have been tightly sealed with energy conservation in mind. On the other hand, the seal on homes varies a great deal. In many warm areas of the country there has been less stress on weatherization and energy efficiency. So if the windows and doors have not been weatherized to fit tightly and you live in a climate where the windows will generally be opened, testing for the

indicator pollutants may not be for you. However, if you
live in a cold climate where the house will be closed up
in winter, and perhaps in summer to run the air
conditioner, you may want to have the indicator pollutant levels checked.

By using a few pollutants—carbon dioxide, carbon
monoxide, and formaldehyde—as general indicators of
overall air quality, the cost of finding out if you have an
indoor air pollution problem is minimized. A visual
inspection, coupled with an inspection for asbestos and
testing for radon, chlordane, carbon dioxide, carbon monoxide, and formaldehyde will not be that expensive and
could save you money and ill health down the line. All
of these tests and inspections should not exceed $1000.
While this may seem expensive, remember as a
homebuyer you are already spending a considerable
amount to have your home inspected for termites and
structural soundness for much the same purpose: to save
money in the long run and to negotiate repairs into the
sale contract. Moreover, the cost pales when compared
with the misery and expense of environmental diseases.

Guidance is provided in subsequent chapters for
choosing a consultant to discover and solve asbestos and
radon problems. General advice on selecting an environmental consultant is given in Chapter Twelve.

How to Solve Indoor Pollution Problems

If you find an indoor air pollution problem don't be
dismayed. There are three basic solutions.

First, **identifying the sources** of indoor air pollution
allows you to eliminate them. Faulty stoves or furnaces
that produce nitrogen dioxide or carbon dioxide can be
fixed or replaced. Leaks that supply mold colonies with
moisture can be repaired. Other materials, such as
asbestos, can be removed or sealed.

A second approach is to **dilute the level** of indoor pollutants by increasing the flow of fresh air. This means
keeping windows open, running kitchen and bathroom
fans, or installing equipment that vents indoor air after
transferring its heat to incoming fresh air. These "heat

recovery ventilators" can be installed either in central air conditioning systems or windows.

A third method is to **purchase air cleaning devices**, which range from inexpensive tabletop models to expensive and complicated whole-house systems. Generally these remove particles from the air, but are not effective on gas pollutants.

You can generally solve indoor air pollution problems without major expense and structural work, except as noted below and in subsequent chapters. Here is some advice on reducing specific pollutants.

Formaldehyde

If your home is new or has urea-formaldehyde insulation, chances are that levels of this pollutant may be higher than average. You can reduce these levels until the materials stop giving off fumes by running an air conditioner or dehumidifier to lower humidity and by increasing ventilation. Whenever you bring in new sources of formaldehyde—including furniture with pressed wood, paneling and plywood—increase ventilation until the product's original odor dissipates.

Combustion Byproducts

You can prevent buildup of nitrogen dioxide, carbon monoxide and other pollutants by:

● Making sure gas or oil heaters and stoves are cleaned and properly adjusted;

● Making sure furnaces are vented to the outdoors;

● Using exhaust fans vented to the outdoors over gas stoves;

● Making sure wood stoves are certified to meet EPA emission standards and have tight fitting doors; and

• Fixing any blocks, leaks, or damage in fireplace flues and chimneys. These flaws can cause inflow of carbon monoxide and other pollutants.

Volatile Organic Compound Fumes

These fumes, known as VOC's, are introduced to the home by products, materials, and use of water, which can contain trace levels of VOC's and chloroform produced by chlorination at the local water treatment plant. To prevent buildup of such vapors:

• Use paints, solvents, waxes, glues and other chemical products only in well ventilated rooms;

• Increase air flow when synthetic carpet is installed and consider having it installed at a time of the year when you can open the windows;

• Store chemical products in an outside shed or well ventilated garage, since they slowly leak fumes into the air;

• Don't purchase chemical products in quantities that will not be used quickly;

• Use cedar wood blocks or lavendar instead of mothballs in woolen trunks;

• Responsibly discard fuels and paint supplies that will not be used immediately, unless they are kept in an outdoor shed.

• Run the bathroom fan or open the window when showering.

Biologicals

Mold, fungi and bacteria grow in damp areas indoors. They are more prevalent in areas with humid climates, where water often condenses on cool surfaces in basements and other areas. Steps to prevent or reduce buildup include:

● Venting clothes dryers to the outdoors to minimize moisture buildup inside;

● Installing and using bathroom and kitchen fans to vent steam;

● Removing, cleaning, and drying wet or damp carpets within 24 hours (**Warning:** once infected, you may want to consider replacement, since disinfection is difficult);

● Regularly emptying water trays in refrigerators, air conditioners, and dehumidifiers;

● Installing vents to keep attics and crawl spaces under the home dry, ideally between 30 and 50 percent humidity;

● Cleaning any humidifiers frequently and using only distilled water to prevent bacteria growth;

● Using a dehumidifier in the basement when humidity is above 50 percent;

● Cleaning and disinfecting the basement floor drain regularly; and

● Patching all basement water leaks and installing outside vents before finishing or using a basement for living space.

To prevent build up of microscopic dust mites, animal dander and pollen, clean frequently. **Warning:** If you are allergic to these substances, have someone else vacuum.

Most of these steps do not require major expenditures and will go a long way toward keeping air healthy in your home. The next few chapters cover the more deadly pollutants.

CHECK LIST FOR HEALTHY INDOOR AIR

Visually Inspect For:

  □ Venting of furnace, water heater, dryer and stove

  □ Venting of attic, basement, and crawl spaces

  □ Proximity of vents to outdoor pollution sources

  □ Exposed foam insulation

  □ Signs of water leaks or condensation

  □ Fireplace flue and chimney blockages, cracks, or leaks

  □ Possible asbestos material

  □ Suspicious odors

  □ Weatherproofing

If Buying, Remember To Ask:

  □ Has the home been treated for termites or other insects?

  □ Is there urea-formaldehyde insulation?

  □ Is any wood stove certified to meet EPA standards

Test For:

☐ Radon (see Chapter Three)

☐ Asbestos (see Chapter Four)

☐ Chlordane (see Chapter Six)

If Weatherproofed In Cold Climate, Consider Testing For:

☐ Carbon Dioxide

☐ Carbon Monoxide

☐ Formaldehyde

MAJOR INDOOR AIR POLLUTANTS

Pollutant	Source	Health Effects
Asbestos	Building materials, including insulation, acoustical ceiling, and pipe wrap	Lung cancer and lung diseases.
Formaldehyde	Foam insulation inside walls, particle board and plywood	Respiratory tract irritation, damage to nostril tissue and cancer.
Radon	Comes from the earth through cracks in the foundation and well water	Lung cancer.
Carbon Monoxide	Gas appliances, fireplaces, kerosene heaters, wood stoves and tobacco smoke	Blocks oxygen flow causing fatigue, then headaches, confusion, nausea, dizziness and death.
Nitrogen Dioxide	Gas appliances, fireplaces and wood stoves	Eye and respiratory tract irritation and infection; long-term exposure causes bronchitis. Diseases characterized by watery eyes, sneezing, lethargy, rashes, coughing, breathing and digestive problems.
Biological Agents	Improperly maintained air ducts, air conditioners, humidifiers, dehumidifiers, carpet and air filters	
Organic Compounds	Cleaners, waxes, paints, pesticides, adhesives, insulation, plywood, furniture, chlorine, moth balls and drycleaned items; autos.	Respiratory tract and eye irritation; many of these cause cancer.
Lead	Paint and auto exhaust	Attacks the nervous system and brain.
Aromatic hydrocarbons	Adhesives, pesticides, paints, cleaners, waxes; heaters, stoves; tobacco; auto exhaust, heating system	Respiratory tract irritation and cancer.

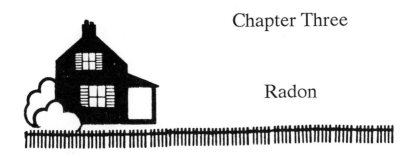

Chapter Three

Radon

A terrifying thing happened to Stanley Watras when he arrived at work one day in 1985. Watras, a nuclear power plant engineer in Boyertown, Pennsylvania, set off alarms as he walked through radiation detectors. At that moment, he realized he had succumbed to the dreaded occupational hazard of nuclear industry workers: radiation poisoning.

How had Watras been contaminated? Were other workers affected? These were among the first questions plant safety and health experts asked.

But in the ensuing investigation, as reported in the *National Law Journal*, it became apparent the plant was not the source of Watras' contamination. Rather, health experts found that Watras had been poisoned in his home. And so was his family. Officials found they had been living in a virtual "radioactive cloud" of odorless, invisible radon gas, which is a potent cause of lung cancer. The air the family had been breathing was as dangerous as smoking an unimagineable 135 packs of cigarettes a day.

Today, the Environmental Protection Agency and Surgeon General warn that radon contamination is so widespread geographically that everyone should test their home for the deadly, but slow-working gas. Indeed, state environmental agencies throughout the country have started radon information programs and in New Jersey, Pennsylvania, and Colorado it is standard practice to disclose radon problems in any home sale contract. (See

Figure 3-1

Major Radon Entry Routes into Your Home

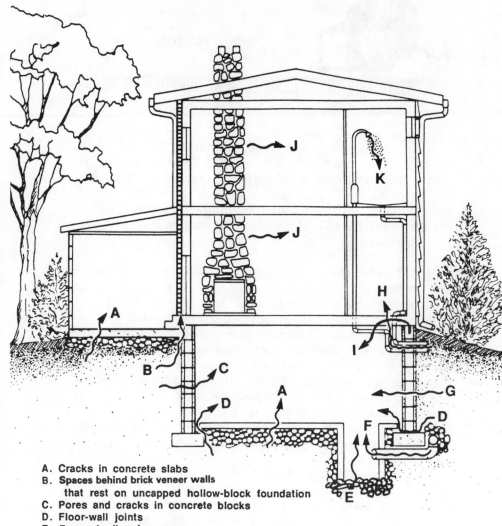

A. Cracks in concrete slabs
B. **Spaces behind brick veneer walls**
   that rest on uncapped hollow-block foundation
C. Pores and cracks in concrete blocks
D. Floor-wall joints
E. **Exposed soil, as in a sump**
F. **Weeping (drain) tile, if drained to open sump**
G. **Mortar joints**
H. Loose fitting pipe penetrations
 I. Open tops of block walls
J. Building materials such as some rock
K. Water (from some wells)

the Appendix for a list of helpful state agencies.)

Radon is given off by radioactive uranium as it decays in the earth and gradually seeps up to the surface and enters the home through cracks, joints, sumps, exposed dirt, water pipes from wells, and other openings. Once inside, radon gas tends to build up since air in the home does not circulate as quickly as outside. **Warning:** radon can also be emitted from building materials, such as stones used in fireplaces.

Buildups generally are worst in winter because homes are kept closed up. Concentrations also can reach high levels, just as with other indoor pollutants, when homes are tightly sealed to conserve energy.

Radioactive radon gas is inhaled and long-term exposure to sufficient concentrations can cause lung cancer. Each year about 130,000 people die of lung cancer, the American Cancer Society estimates. While the overwhelming majority get it from smoking, the number who contract it from radon is still quite significant. EPA estimates the gas causes between 5,000 and 20,000 lung cancer deaths a year in the United States.

Health Risks from Radon

The chances of getting lung cancer from radon depend upon the concentration in your home. EPA estimates risk from exposure at any given level based on living in a home for 70 years and spending 75 percent of your time there. If you spend more time at home, the risk goes up. Conversely, if you spend less, the risk goes down.

Radon is measured in units called picocuries per cublic liter of air. When concentrations over four picocuries per liter are detected, EPA recommends corrective action to reduce levels. Here are EPA's estimates of lung cancer risk at various radon levels:

Radon Concentration	Risk Per 100 People
4 Picocuries/Liter Air	Between 1 and 5
20 Picocuries/Liter Air	Between 6 and 21
200 Picocuries/Liter Air	Between 44 and 77

At a concentration of 200 picocuries per liter, EPA warns that even if you live in a home for only 10 years your chances of developing lung cancer are still high at between 14 and 42 per 100.

Put another way, when exposed to radon concentrations in the range of 200 picocuries per liter you run the same risk of getting lung cancer as someone who smokes four packs of cigarettes a day. Exposure to a concentration of 20 picocuries per liter poses a risk equivalent to smoking between one and two packs a day.

The risk at any concentration is higher for smokers since radon compounds the risk of lung cancer. It also is higher for children, since they are more sensitive than adults to toxics and radioactivity. And those who sleep in a basement are liable to be exposed to radon levels that are even higher than those on the first or second floor of a home.

Warning: If you think your risk will be significantly lowered because you plan to stay in a home for a limited period of time, remember you may have been exposed to high levels of radon in previous homes before environmental scientists recognized the threat. Moreover, you may be exposed in a future dwelling too. Therefore, it is wise to check for radon wherever you live and take corrective action if there is a problem. It is also wise to check for radon before purchasing a home and to negotiate any necessary corrective steps into the contract. Tips on negotiating are offered in Chapter Twelve.

How to Measure For Radon

Fortunately, since radon was first raised as a major environmental health threat in the mid-1980's, testing has become easy and inexpensive. Radon test kits are readily available at supermarkets and hardware stores in most areas. The two most widely used and least expensive kits are the carbon canister, which costs $10 to $25, and the Alpha-track detector, which costs $20 to $50. The price includes analysis, which is done by mailing the kits into a

Figure 3-2

Measuring for Radon

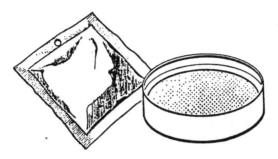

Charcoal Canisters
Test Period: 3 to 7 days
Approximate Cost: $10 to $25 for one canister

Alpha Track Detectors
Minimum Test Period: 2 to 4 weeks
Approximate Cost: $20 to $50 for one
detector; discounts for multiple detectors

laboratory. Results are returned via mail.

The carbon canister kit is filled with activated charcoal, which absorbs radon out of the air. The canister is exposed in your home for three to seven days and then sent to the laboratory, which counts the Gamma rays emitted as the radon decays.

The Alpha-track detector is a small piece of plastic which collects the tracks of Alpha particles, also emitted as radon decays. This device must be exposed in the home for between two and four weeks. Afterwards it is sent to the lab, which counts the Alpha particle tracks.

EPA recommends a two-step protocol for using these devices. Step one, known as the screening measurement, is intended to provide a quick answer to whether you have a radon problem. It calls for putting a test kit in the lowest living area of your home, namely the basement if there is one, after having the windows closed for at least 12 hours. During the test kit exposure period, keep the windows and doors closed as much as possible. It is best to conduct the screening test during the cool months of the year, since the house will be closed anyway.

The screening measurement is unlikely to give you an accurate picture of the average radon level, but it is a good indicator of whether further measurements are needed, including in other rooms in your home, such as those upstairs. If necessary, in step two of the radon diagnosis procedure you should follow up by exposing several kits and averaging their readings together to get a better idea of the seriousness of any problem.

EPA's guidelines for interpreting the first-step screening test results are:

• If the level is 200 picocuries per liter or higher, conduct followup measurements immediately, exposing test kits over a one-week period during which the windows and doors remain closed as much as possible. Also consider taking action to redue the radon level.

Figure 3-3

Natural Ventilation

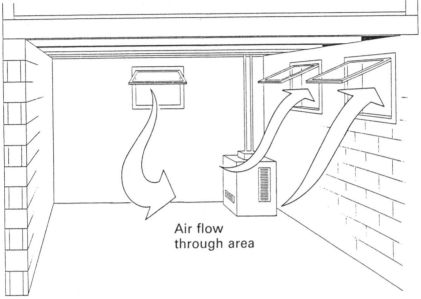

Air flow
through area

Figure 3-4

Forced Air Ventilation

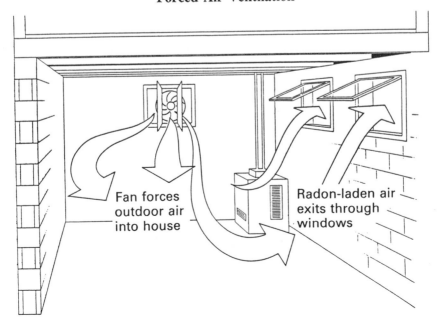

Fan forces
outdoor air
into house

Radon-laden air
exits through
windows

• If the level is between 20 and 200 picocuries per liter, followup measurements should be conducted, with test kits exposed over a three-month period during which the windows and doors are closed as much as possible.

• If the level is between four and 20 picocuries per liter, then do further measurements, including exposing test kits for one year, or exposing detectors for one week in each of four seasons.

• If the level is below four picocuries per liter and the house was closed as much as possible before and during the test, relax, there is little chance of a radon problem.

Other radon measurement methods are available and there are firms that will conduct tests. These methods are:

□ **Continuous monitoring**, which uses an electronic detector for a six- or 24-hour period;

□ **Radon progeny integrating sampling**, which uses a pump to pull air through detectors; and

□ **Radon grab sampling**, which consists of collecting air in a special flask.

The advantage of these for the homebuyer is their quick turnaround compared with the carbon canister and Alpha-track detector methods. These other methods, however, generally require skilled technicians. EPA maintains a list of qualified radon test firms. Details on obtaining that list are given in the Appendix.

If subsequent measurements are above four picocuries per liter, you should take action to reduce the concentration of radon.

How to Solve Radon Problems

When followup measurements show the radon level is

200 picocuries or greater, EPA recommends immediate corrective action. When it is between 20 and 200 picocuries, action should be taken within months. Between four and 20 picocuries, action should be taken within a few years.

Investment-free options for reducing your exposure to radon include spending less time in areas with high levels, keeping windows open and window fans on to maximize ventilation, and if there is a crawl space under the house, keeping the vents on all sides of the home open all year long. EPA warns, however, that natural ventilation will not effectively reduce radon concentrations above 40 picocuries per liter. Further, keeping windows open will increase heating and cooling costs.

Another factor is to make sure that the air pressure in your home is not lower than the air pressure in the soil. When it is, your house draws in radon. Depressurization can result from having windows open only on the downwind side, using exhaust fans in bathrooms, the kitchen, and attic, and using furnaces and clothes dryers. Sometimes the cause is more complicated.

Other options for reducing radon can range from less than $100 to several thousand dollars. Some states have or are considering financial aid programs to help homeowners correct radon problems. Pennsylvania, for instance, offers low cost loans. Check the Appendix to find out how to get information about any programs in your state.

The other corrective measures include:

● **Patching cracks** and openings through which radon enters the home;

● **Installing ventilation fans,** which can be coupled with heat exchangers to capture and reuse heat from inside air before it is ventilated to the outside;

● Bringing a direct air supply to appliances that use air—such as woodstoves, fireplaces, furnaces, and clothes dryers—to reduce the degree to which they depressurize your home;

• **Covering and venting** to the outside exposed areas of earth in your basement, such as sumps; and

• **Suction systems,** consisting of pipes that can run under your home or through the basement walls to collect radon before it has a chance to enter.

If your home has a drain-tile system—perforated pipes that run around it to collect and divert water—this can be modified to collect radon as well.

These methods generally are 90 percent efficient in reducing radon, except for covering cracks and openings, covering and venting exposed earth, and supplying air to appliances, which are site specific in their radon reduction efficiency. Suction methods generally are at least 97 percent efficient, but are expensive to install.

When radon enters a home through water, a problem that occurs particularly with private wells and small community well systems serving subdivisions, it can be eliminated in two ways. The water can be aerated outdoors to release radon before it enters the home or can be filtered with granular activated carbon.

In choosing a contractor for corrective action, be sure to contact the radon office in your state (see the Appendix), obtain competitive bids, check references, and enter a written contract that protects you should the project not reduce radon as represented. Definitely conduct followup measurements after work has been completed. Tips on dealing with contractors are covered in Chapter Eleven.

Figure 3-5

Patching Cracks

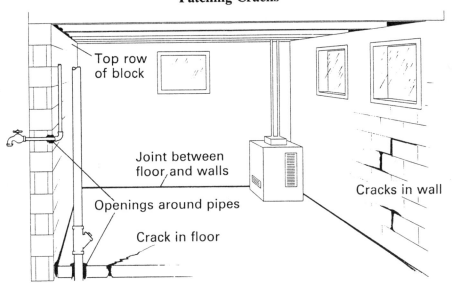

Figure 3-6

Outside Fan

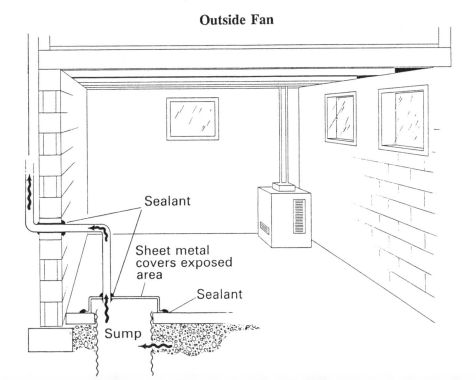

CHECK LIST FOR RADON

To Check For Radon:

☐ Expose detector in **lowest level** of home

☐ If level is high, retest in several rooms

When Levels Are Elevated:

☐ **Seal** all **cracks** and joints

☐ Eliminate negative air pressure

☐ **Leave windows open,** on upwind and downwind side of house, not just on downwind side.

☐ Bring direct air supply from outside using fan.

☐ Cover and ventilate open areas of earth in basement to outside.

☐ Recheck levels.

☐ If levels are still high:

☐ Install forced ventilation fans with heat exchangers.

☐ Contact a consultant about a suction system.

Chapter Four

Asbestos

A 1969 meeting between Clarence Borel and attorney Ward Stephenson marked the beginning of a legal odyssey that eventually rocked corporate America and helped bring landmark legislation and regulation. Borel, an asbestos worker, was short of breath when he arrived at Stephenson's law offices in the East Texas town of Orange. The pale and emaciated 57-year old told the attorney his tragic story. Borel, whose story was reported in The New Yorker, had worked with asbestos since 1936 until he experienced pain in the right side of his chest and hard breathing in 1969. Medical exams ending in exploratory surgery revealed a lung disease known as asbestosis. Doctors found asbestos fibers embedded in his lung tissue.

Stephenson filed suit on Borel's behalf, charging the Johns-Manville Products Corp. and other firms with failure to warn of the dangers of asbestos. Borel never lived to see the outcome of the suit, in which a jury found the defendants liable for damages. He died June 3, 1970, after doctors removed one afflicted lung. But the legal precedent set in the case gave way to a flood of asbestos worker suits that led Johns Manville to seek protection by filing for bankruptcy in 1982. By doing so, the company limited future suits and set up a $2 billion trust fund to pay off worker claims.

As a home owner or buyer, chances are low you will ever suffer exposure to asbestos levels as high as those encountered regularly by Borel and other asbestos workers. Yet many environmental scientists believe a single high-level exposure to asbestos can cause long-term respiratory disease. And indeed, environmental officials have worked to eradicate asbestos hazards not only in industry, but in public buildings and consumer products. The 1970's saw occupational standards for asbestos workers and bans on using the fibrous material in such products as pipe covering, artificial fireplace logs, and hair dryers. In 1984, EPA issued standards for renovating and demolishing buildings with asbestos materials. Later in 1986, Congress required the nation's schools to take action on asbestos, including regular inspections and removal or encapsulation of damaged asbestos. Congress also required EPA and states to accredit asbestos inspectors and contractors.

Yet after 20 years of litigation and regulation, the law is still silent on asbestos in the home, even though much of the 30 million tons of asbestos mined in the U.S. since the turn of the century remains in homes today.

Consumption of asbestos peaked at 800,000 tons a year in the early 1970's and has declined by 70 percent since then due to health concerns. Long-known for its resistance to fire and corrosion, asbestos has been used for insulation and building materials since the early 1900's. Contractors, particularly between World War II and the mid-1960's, used a variety of asbestos-containing materials in homebuilding. Asbestos was commonly used in:

- Vinyl **floor tiles** and vinyl sheet flooring;

- **Wall patching compounds** and textured paints;

- **Acoustical ceiling insulation,** applied with either a sprayer or trowel;

- **Insulation** used around wood-burning stoves to protect the floor and walls from heat;

- **Furnace insulation,** including door gaskets on wood and coal stoves;

- **Insulation on** hot water and steam heating **pipes** and behind walls and ceilings;

• **Appliances**, such as **ovens**, ranges, refrigerators, and **dryers**; and

• **Roofing shingles**, siding shingles, and siding sheets.

Some of these materials, such as insulation, are 80 or 90 percent asbestos, while others, such as floor tile or roofing, are about 20 percent asbestos. Likewise, some are more likely to release asbestos and create a toxic threat in the home. In general, asbestos insulation such as pipe wrap, ceiling coating, roofing felts and gaskets are likely to release asbestos. Other products, such as floor tile and cement asbestos shingles and sheet board, are less likely to release asbestos except when being sawed, sanded or drilled.

Figure 4-1

Relative Size of Asbestos Particles

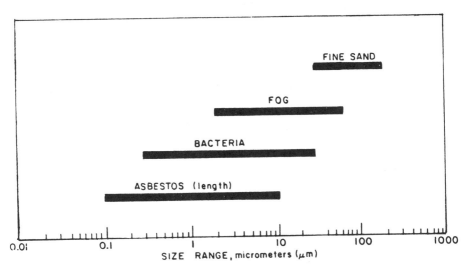

Exposure and Health Effects

When building materials containing asbestos crumble they can release asbestos fibers into the air. These fibers are generally so small they are invisible and like fog, fine sand, and bacteria remain in the air for hours before settling. When the fibers settle, they are easily stirred up into the air again.

Inhaling asbestos is the primary health threat. The small fibers evade the respiratory system's natural defenses to find their way deep into the lungs. At once they reach the lung tissue, the fibers become embedded and can cause a variety of fatal illnesses. Moreover, environmental health scientists warn studies so far show there is no known exposure level that is safe. Inhaling asbestos fibers even once can lead to fatal lung disease. But it takes time for asbestos to cause illness, about 20 years or more in most people.

One of the leading health studies on asbestos, conducted by the National Institute of Occupational Safety and Health, indicated that people exposed to the fiber had five times the chance of developing fatal lung diseases as those not exposed. Moreover, exposed smokers were found to be 50 times more likely to develop lung cancer than unexposed smokers. Asbestos is considered so dangerous that workers who handle it or products containing the material are required to wear sophisticated respirators.

Asbestos has been found to cause:

- **Asbestosis,** a non-cancerous scarring of the lungs that causes shortness or breath and a dry crackling sound in the lungs during inhalation. In its advanced form, this disease can cause cardiac failure and death.

- **Mesothelioma,** a rare cancer of the thin membrane lining of the chest and abdomen. The earlier in life asbestos is inhaled, the greater the chance of later developing mesothelioma, which is nearly always fatal.

- **Lung cancer**, which can be caused by asbestos even in the absence of asbestosis.

Some health studies suggest asbestos may also cause cancer of the esophagus, larnyx, oral cavity, stomach, colon and kidneys. Asbestos inhaled into the lungs may be transported to these other organs by the bloodstream.

While any exposure to asbestos can cause such diseases, not everyone who is exposed falls ill. Consider the National Institute for Occupational Safety and Health study, which examined the causes of death among 17,500 asbestos insulation workers. The institute found that ten in 1,000 died of asbestosis, less than 30 per 1,000 of lung cancer, less than 15 in 1,000 of mesothelioma, and less than 20 in 1,000 of other types of cancer.

Asbestos is clearly a health hazard, but exposure levels at home are far lower in the vast majority of cases than in asbestos-related industries. One study Mount Sinai School of Medicine conducted in Orange County, California, for instance, found extremely low levels of airborne asbestos in a sample of tract homes that had heating ducts wrapped with asbestos insulation and acoustical ceilings containing asbestos. Followup studies of homes with damaged asbestos conducted by the Consumer Product Safety Commission found low levels as well. But if you are not comforted by such studies, have your home inspected.

How to Find and Solve Asbestos Problems

Asbestos presents a health hazard when it is crumbling or has the potential to crumble, a state known as friable. If you are living in or purchasing any house built before the mid-1970's, have it examined for friable asbestos material and any other material that has the potential to release asbestos.

An inspection should be performed by a professional asbestos contractor. This contractor should inspect materials in your house to determine which may contain asbestos and should sample those materials according to EPA-designated procedures for laboratory analysis to confirm asbestos is present. A thorough inspection should cost around 5 cents per square foot of house.

The contractor should check walls, ceilings, insulated pipes, boilers, and furnaces. He also should look behind any dropped ceilings or partitions. Any friable material or exposed insulation should be sampled and analyzed. All unexposed pipe and boiler insulation should be assumed to contain asbestos.

Should the inspection show that asbestos is present, the question then is what should be done. When the material is stable, shows no sign of deterioration, and is unlikely to be disturbed except through work then it is best to leave it alone. **Warning:** asbestos can be released not only by deterioration of the asbestos-containing material itself, but also when the material under it deteriorates. For instance, leaks from above that destroy ceiling plaster covered with asbestos accoustical coating can cause release of fibers.

When asbestos is in a friable state it should be attended to. The basic choices are either to remove it altogether or to encapsulate it with a covering that will seal it from the air. Removal should average about $15 per square foot of asbestos material and the cost of encapsulation will depend upon the job. Leave stable asbestos material alone, but monitor its condition and have it attended to should it become friable.

How to Deal With Contractors

Asbestos removal or encapsulation is not a job for amateurs. It requires specialized equipment and adherence to detailed procedures specified by EPA. Therefore, the most important step you can take as a homeowner or prospective homebuyer is to do a good job of selecting a contractor for any asbestos-related problems. (See Chapter Eleven for general advice on dealing with contractors).

EPA advises that in dealing with contractors you:

● Require evidence of experience and employee **training certificates** in asbestos removal. Many states require certification of contractors.

● Require **written proof of** adequate liability **insurance.**

□ Ask for copies of standard operating procedures.

□ Make sure you get a **written bid** outlining exactly what the asbestos related problems are and how they will be remedied.

□ Obtain **several bids. Warning:** Select the best qualified contractor, not the least expensive, or you could be asking for trouble and greater expense in the long-run.

□ **Avoid contracting in the summer** if possible, because asbestos contractors are often overtaxed and hurried in doing remedial work at schools when they are out of session.

□ Always **check references,** including others the contractor has worked for.

□ When the job is done, make sure the contractor does a thorough **visual inspection** to insure that cleanup is adequate.

□ **Warning: Double-check the adequacy of cleanup** by having someone who is not employed by the contractor conduct air monitoring.

Abestos removal work is governed by EPA standards, except on houses and small buildings, which generally are exempt. Nevertheless, it is also a good idea to ask the contractor to provide a list of any violations of standards and how those violations were resolved.

Following these steps will help insure that your home is free of asbestos problems.

CHECK LIST FOR ASBESTOS

Signs of Trouble:

□ Deteriorating acoustical ceiling

□ Deteriorating insulation wrap around pipes and air ducts

□ Deteriorating door gaskets on wood stoves

□ Deteriorating insulation on furnaces, water heaters and clothes dryers

□ Damaged floor or roof tiles

□ Damaged exterior wall shingles or panels

□ Deteriorating insulation in walls or attics

Remember:

□ Have a professional inspect your home for friable or potentially friable asbestos material.

□ Have a professional contractor either remove or encapsulate friable asbestos.

□ **Do not attempt to do asbestos work yourself.**

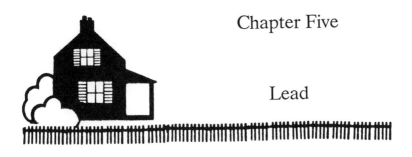

Chapter Five

Lead

In October 1985 Judy Southerland and her husband Maurice Sanders became concerned when their twin infants were not growing as fast as other babies their age. One of their girls was just 50 percent of normal size and suffered from chronic constipation and despondence.

Alarmed, the couple sought medical help. Their pediatrician found the twins had very high levels of lead in their blood, 37 and 34 micrograms per liter respectively. A level of 25 micrograms per liter constitutes lead poisoning, the U.S. Public Health Service says and adverse effects have been observed at levels as low as 10 micrograms per liter.

After hearing the test results, the couple asked city health officials to check their home in the comfortably affluent Palisades section of Washington, D.C., to find the source of the lead. At first, the D.C. Commission on Public Health suspected the paint. Eventually, however, a private testing firm retained by the couple, whose story was reported in the Washington Post, found lead in the home's drinking water at almost eight times the level allowed under the Environmental Protection Agency's standard of 20 parts per billion.

Lead has long been recognized by public health officials as one of the most pernicious and widespread contaminants in the environment. It is found in small amounts in virtually all soil, food, water and air and is routinely ingested and inhaled. As long as the total dose is low, it poses no threat. But man-made sources of lead often compound doses to dangerous levels.

Figure 5-1

Pathways of Lead to Humans

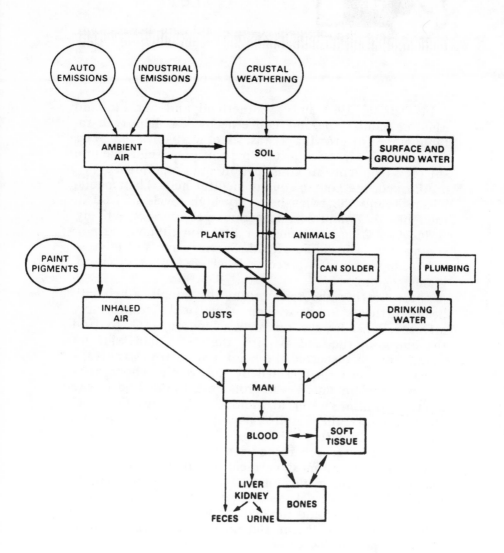

Too much lead damages the brain, central nervous system, kidneys and red blood cells. In adults, lead can also cause hypertension, strokes and heart attacks. In children, lead can stunt growth and mental development, often first manifesting itself as learning disability in grade school. Pregnant women exposed to high levels of lead can damage the health of their yet born infants. Rapidly growing fetuses and young children absorb lead more readily. Moreover, a small dose of lead for an adult can be a comparatively large dose for a small body.

Recognizing the danger, the government has done much to cut the amount of lead introduced into the environment by humans, including requiring cars that run on unleaded fuel, phasing down the lead content of regular gasoline for older autos, eliminating leaded house paint, and requiring pollution controls on lead smelters.

Yet, lead continues to be a major environmental problem with children all too frequently suffering low intelligence quotients and other effects of lead poisoning. EPA has renewed its concern over lead with a recent warning that some 40 million Americans get too much of the toxic metal in their drinking water. The contaminant leaches into water out of lead in household plumbing and water distribution systems.

In urban areas with busy thoroughfares and old neighborhoods where homes were once coated with leaded paint, contaminated soil can increase the lead dosage for children. Most of the lead emitted by autos running on leaded gasoline both today and especially in the past has landed on the soil within a few hundred feet of the roadway. Lead paint chipped off homes during repainting and weathered by the elements winds up in the yard below. **Warning:** these factors may have in effect created a major reservoir of lead in the yard around your dream home. Moreover, most of this lead is probably in the top inch of the soil, the layer that is tracked into the home, enters the air as dust when it is windy, and comes into contact with children at play.

As a homeowner or prospective buyer, you need to be concerned about lead in the drinking water, paint, and soil in the yard. Lead should be of particular concern if you have or plan to have children. And you should dispel any notion that lead is a problem confined to poor inner city areas. A 1988 report to Congress by the federal A- gency for Toxic Substances and Disease Registry in At- lanta concluded that lead is "pervasive toxic" affecting children "in all socioeconomic/demographic strata." Des- pite past regulatory actions, the center said, "At present, little or no margin of safety exists between existing lead levels in large segments of the U.S. population and those levels associated with toxicity risk." Lead levels in the general environment are so high that whenever you or your children come into contact with lead contamination at home, lead in your blood can quickly reach toxic concentrations.

Among the other important conclusions outlined in the report:

  • **Twelve million children** under seven years of age **are exposed to potentially toxic levels of lead paint** in the home. Lead in homes "remains an untouched and enormously serious problem despite some regulatory action in the early 1970's to limit further input of new leaded paint to the environment. For this source, corrective actions have been a clear failure."

  • Some 400,000 fetuses are exposed to high levels of lead each year and over ten years this means **four million infants** are likely to be **born with lead poisoning.**

  • **Lead will remain an environmental health problem** for a long time, because it is an element that cannot be destroyed. The only way to minimize its effects is by ef- fectively managing exposure.

Here then is a guide to managing exposure in an around your home.

Lead in Drinking Water

Environmental scientists became concerned about lead

in drinking water in the mid-1980's. Studies showed persistent lead poisoning in children long after the metal had been virtually eliminated from gasoline and in areas without lead paint and soil contamination. After substantial analysis of the problem, EPA in 1987 estimated that 40 million Americans drink and cook with tap water that contains excessive levels of the toxic metal.

Lead pipes and solder in both water distribution systems and household plumbing **are the source of the contamination.** In homes built before 1930, lead service connection pipes, running from the house to the water main, are frequently found. Pipes containing lead used to ground household electrical devices, such as telephones, will introduce lead into water too.

Lead leaches out of the pipes and solder when water is left standing for several hours. The longer water stands, the higher the lead level. Corrosive water—increasingly found in the Northeast and other areas of country that suffer from acid rain—compounds the leaching phenomenon. Areas of the country with soft water—which is low in dissolved mineral content—are also prone to high lead levels, according to EPA, as are households in high mineral areas that soften their water through treatment.

How to Find Lead Contamination

In light of health studies showing lead in drinking water presents a major health problem, EPA recently lowered its standard for the toxic metal from 50 parts per billion to 20 parts per billion. Whenever lead occurs in tap water above 20 parts per billion, a person should take steps to guard against lead poisoning, particularly if there are children or infants in the household.

To find out if tap water contains too much lead, it should be sampled and analyzed by a laboratory. In many states, the law requires local water system operators to analyze water samples for contaminants free of charge. So check with your water utility before retaining a private laboratory.

Two water samples should be drawn and placed in

containers provided or specified by the testing laboratory. **Warning:** Be exact in following the laboratory's
instructions, otherwise your test results could be marred.
Generally, a "first draw" sample should be taken after the
water has not been used in the house for several hours. A
second "fully flushed" sample should be taken after the
water has run for several minutes.

Definitely test water for lead in homes that are either
very old or less than five years old. Lead pipes were frequently used in older homes and can be detected by their
dull grey color and soft surface that can be easily scrat-
ched with a key. Lead solder was commonly used to join
copper pipes until Congress banned it in 1986. After
about five years of use, the solder generally becomes covered by a mineral coating that prevents further leaching
of lead. However, this coating does not form when the
water is corrosive or soft. A lead analysis also should be
conducted whenever there are frequent leaks, rust-color-
ed water, or stained laundry and dishes.

If a private laboratory is used for water analysis, make
sure it is approved by EPA or the state (see the
Appendix for further information). An analysis of lead
should run between $30 and $100.

Solving a Lead in Water Problem

If analysis reveals a level of 20 parts per billion or
greater of lead in tap water it is necessary to take protec-
tive steps.

The first should be to let the water run until you feel
its temperature drop whenever it has not been used for
more than six hours, such as first thing in the morning or
when you first arrive home from work. This will flush
the water that has remained in the household pipes long
enough to absorb lead. If you flush this water into a
basin, you can use it for dishwashing or other non-
drinking purposes rather than wasting it. After flushing
the system, fill a few jugs of water and store them in the
refrigerator for drinking. This will minimize the need to
flush later. **Warning: never use hot water for cooking or**

drinking, **especially when making infant formula, because
hot water dissolves lead more easily than cold.** Also, if you
live in a high rise or large apartment complex with lead
in the plumbing, it is almost impossible to adequately
flush the system.

Provided that your fully flushed sample shows a level
well below 20 parts per billion, flushing may be all you
need to protect yourself against lead poisoning. However,
if the fully flushed sample has a level near or greater
than 20 parts per billion, it is wise to take further action.
This includes a range of steps, from purchasing bottled
water and training youngsters to drink it exclusively, to
replacing lead pipes.

New EPA regulations require drinking water suppliers
to adjust the acidity of water to minimize its ability to
dissolve lead. However, it will take time before the
requirement is fully enforced. Moreover if you have a
private well or water supply, or get your water from a
very small system, EPA's regulation will not help. In this
case, short of removing the lead pipes, home treatment
will be necessary and there are two basic methods.

In the first, a calcite filter is placed between the water
supply and any pipes in household plumbing that contain
lead. This method eliminates the corrosive character of
the water so it does not dissolve lead with which it comes
into contact.

The second treatment method is to use a reverse
osmosis unit. This device should only be installed at the
tap since it softens the water. In reverse osmosis, water
molecules, which are relatively small, pass through holes
in a sheet of material and lead and other larger molecules too big for the holes are left behind. Water soften-
ed before it reaches the tap will readily dissolve any lead
it comes into contact with, particularly when it is left
standing overnight in the pipes. Osmosis and distillation
devices vary greatly in their effectiveness and need
regular servicing. Before purchasing one, make sure the
installer demonstrates its effectiveness at removing lead
and offers a proper maintenance plan.

When moving into a home it is wise to remove stainers
from the faucets and flush the water for 15 minutes or

more. This will help remove loose chunks of lead from the system. This procedure should be repeated periodically.

Finally, your local water utility or health department is a good source of information when it comes to lead in water. Do not hesitate to call for tips on suppliers of treatment devices, data on how water is being treated to prevent contamination, and data on the location of lead pipes in the system.

Lead in Paint

Leaded paint was used widely inside and outside homes until 1973 and was not actually banned until 1977. Leaded paint was favored because of its perpetual fresh-painted look. With leaded paint, the top surface constantly wears away instead of staying in place to become dirty. Until non-leaded house paints were widely marketed in 1950, virtually all homes were painted with leaded paint.

The problem of leaded paint is so serious that the Department of Housing and Urban Development in 1987 adopted rules requiring repair of any defective paint before the sale of any pre-1973 house with FHA mortgage insurance. FHA receives about two million mortgage insurance applications a year on pre-1973 homes and approves about one million. Under HUD's rules, the appraiser for FHA must inspect all interior and exterior surfaces up to five feet from the floor or ground for cracking, scaling, chipping, peeling, or loose paint. These surfaces, which children are likely to come into contact with, include the walls, stairs, decks, porches, railings, windows and doors. If the appraiser finds defective paint, it is up to the seller of the home to repair it in accordance with the rules.

HUD says that simply washing and repainting the walls is not sufficient. Rather, paint must either be removed or covered with gypsum wall board or fiberglass cloth. Wall paper can be used if it is permanently attached and not easily strippable. Where paint must be removed, from wood trim and windows for instance, the rules call for scraping or using chemicals or heat treatment with infrared or coil type heat guns. Sanding machines and propane torches are prohibited for removing paint.

If you already live in a home, you can get the paint tested for lead in a laboratory or with a portable X-ray fluoresence analyzer, although it may be more expensive than repairs. There are only about 400 X-ray analyzers in the country, although some are owned by local health departments in major cities. Health departments also will sometimes do lab analysis for lead problems. Private testing with an X-ray analyzer is about $25 per room. Private laboratory analysis is much more expensive at about $175 per room. Several paint samples must be taken in each room. Because of this expense and the limited capacity to test homes for lead paint, HUD found it easier to simply require that damaged paint be removed or covered. As a home owner or buyer, you probably will too.

Lead in Soil

Lead gets into soil from three major sources in residential neighborhoods: chipped paint, auto exhaust, and any nearby lead smelters. Lead in soil is a problem for children who tend to ingest dirt when they play.

While EPA has set no specific "action level" for lead in soil, Minnesota has set a standard of 500 parts per million. The Agency for Toxic Substances and Disease Registry recommends an action level of 1,000 parts per million. Action levels are the basis for deciding when to cleanup contaminated soil under Superfund, the nation's $8.5 billion hazardous waste cleanup program. EPA has found that the average minimum lead level in Superfund site cleanups is around 800 parts per million.

In Boston, the city's Department of Health and Hospitals found lead concentrations averaged 2,000 parts per million around the foundations of old homes with flaking paint. EPA says that each increase of 1,000 parts per million for lead in soil will increase blood lead levels up to 9 micrograms per liter. The average blood lead level in the U.S. is between 7.5 and 15 micrograms per liter, according to the Public Health Service.

Analyzing soil for lead is a complicated and expensive job because the heavy metal is not necessarily distributed evenly. Some areas may have little if any and other areas may have a great deal. Generally, the highest levels are found within six feet of the house when paint is the primary source. But to get an accurate picture of a lead contamination problem several soil samples must be taken from different points on the property and then analyzed in the laboratory, the expense of which was noted above.

You may want to forgo dealing with lead in soil if you do not have young children, especially under six years old. Also, if your home is relatively new and is not located near any thoroughfare it is unlikely there is a problem. But if you do have young children and the home is old or near a thoroughfare you may be safe to assume that the soil is contaminated and consider taking corrective action. Check with your local health department to see if they have information concerning lead contamination of soil in your neighborhood.

How to Deal With Lead in Soil

EPA has a pilot program under way in Boston and other Northeast cities to examine the feasibility of addressing lead soil contamination in residential neighborhoods. The agency recently analyzed five approaches to cleaning up lead contamination in residential yards that have been tested in Boston. EPA's cost estimate for each method is based on addressing the top three inches of soil over an area of 1,456 square feet. Labor and materials are included. All soil should be wet when handled to prevent blowing dust and care should be taken not to track lead contaminated soil into the house. Here is a synopsis of EPA's experience.

• Method: Removing and **disposing of top soil offsite,** bringing in clean soil and revegetating. Effectiveness: Reduces lead level sufficiently. Cost: $1,127. **Caution:** Make sure new soil is clean.

• Method: Removing and **disposing of soil in an onsite pit** covered with two feet of clean soil and revegetating. Effectiveness: Reduces lead level sufficiently. Cost: $791. **Caution:** Contaminated soil could be dug up or brought to the surface by freezing and thawing in the future.

• Method: Covering with six inches of uncontaminated top soil and revegetating, a technique commonly known as **capping.** Effectiveness: Temporarily reduces lead level. Cost $726. **Caution:** Contaminated soil is likely to be brought to the surface by children digging and by the freeze and thaw cycle.

• Method: Removing, decontaminating and placing soil onsite and then revegetating. Effectiveness: Removes 99 percent of lead. Cost: Unknown, but very expensive because it involves chemical treatment in special equipment. **Caution:** This alternative may be applicable to large-scale waste sites, but not individual homes.

• Method: **Rototilling** soil and revegetating. Effectiveness: May help where lead levels are around 500 parts per million, but probably will not be adequate where levels are higher. Cost: $336. **Caution:** This method does not eliminate lead from the surface soil.

One final note of caution. If your neighborhood has a general soil contamination problem, eliminating lead on your property alone will offer just limited protection, since your children may play in other yards. However, combined with other steps to reduce lead from water and paint you will be well on your way to effectively managing lead exposure.

CHECKLIST FOR LEAD

Examine For:

☐ Cracked, peeling, flaking, disintegrating paint on houses built before 1973

☐ Lead in tap water, by having first draw and flushed samples analyzed in the laboratory

☐ With old houses and along thoroughfares, consider whether to test for lead in the soil; check with the local health department for information on lead in your area

If There Is a Problem:

☐ In Water:

☐ Flush pipes before drawing drinking or cooking water if the flushed sample met the EPA standard.

☐ Drink bottled water.

☐ If the level is high after flushing, consider a treatment device or removing any lead pipes.

☐ With Paint:

☐ Remove and cover damaged paint according to FHA rules on homes built before 1973.

☐ In Soil:

☐ Take action to remove surface soil and replace with clean soil and new vegetation.

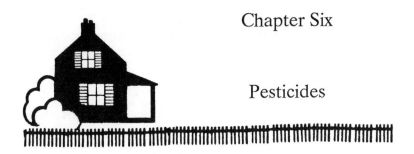

Chapter Six

Pesticides

Christine Carpenter was "happy as a lark" in her suburban Washington, D.C., townhome when she retired in 1985 after 25 years as a secretary. She relished leisurely days in the three-story, four-bedroom townhouse she had bought seven years earlier. It was her sanctuary and a good investment too. In the hot real estate market of the nation's capital, it had already doubled in value.

But then one day in early spring, Carpenter found termites in the living room so she called in exterminators. Soon they were boring holes in the foundation and injecting the pesticide chlordane into the soil underneath, which is generally home to the wood-eating insects.

When they left, Carpenter found white foam on the basement floor. She cleaned it up, but suddenly became tired. In the ensuing months, her health declined rapidly. "I thought I was falling apart from old age," she told the *Washington Post*, which reported her story. "The way I was feeling, I knew I was going to end up in a wheelchair, and I cried." She felt exhausted, her spinal cord was numb, her joints ached. She had trouble breathing and suffered headaches and muscle spasms. Her memory failed and she often felt disoriented or anxious.

Then one day she saw a television news report on the dangers of termite treatments. She later found out her symptoms matched those of chlordane poisoning so she had air samples taken. The results showed her home had a chlordane level more than eight times higher than recommended by the National Academy of Sciences. In effect, Carpenter was being poisoned in the comfort of her own home.

Carpenter moved to a rented apartment after finding it would cost more than $40,000 to decontaminate the home. While her health continued to decline, she began working as a temporary secretary to keep up with her rent and the mortgage for a house she could neither live in or sell.

Carpenter's story is not unique and most of the victims who sued the manufacturer of chlordane, Velsicol Chemical Corp., for damages never got a dime. But eventually, problems with chlordane and heptachlor, a similar insecticide, forced Velsicol to withdraw the products from the market under a 1987 agreement with the Environmental Protection Agency. The pesticides were used for 40 years to treat 30 million American homes for termites and were withdrawn from the market after it became evident there was no safe way to apply them to a home.

But the problems discovered with these two insecticides may be just the tip of the pesticide iceberg. Each year, EPA estimates almost 2,000 people are admitted to U.S. hospitals for acute pesticide poisoning in non-occupational settings. Moreover, pesticides have been widely implicated as a cause of cancer, sterility and birth defects. The National Academy of Sciences estimates that pesticide residue on food alone causes 20,000 cancers a year in the U.S. But that is just a fraction of the cancer risk because the academy has concluded that the greatest exposure stems from pesticide use in urban environments, particularly in the home.

Doubtful? Each year between 300 million and 400 million pounds of active pesticide ingredients are used in the U.S. off the farm. EPA says that over 90 percent of U.S. households use pesticides. In Los Angeles, homeowners are the chief customers of exterminating firms, accounting for about half their revenues. Apartments account for 25 percent of exterminating revenues with the remainder from the workplace, restaurants and other facilities. One Los Angeles exterminator said homeowners generally have preventive spraying or crack and crevice dusting done once a month. "Some people are deathly afraid of seeing an insect anywhere," he said.

"They see a spider and they go into orbit." Of the treatments, he explained, "It's peace of mind and we guarantee it."

About 60 percent of the exterminating industry's $2.7 billion a year in revenue nationwide is for killing roaches, fleas, ants and other small insects. Exterminators treat roaches with diazanon and dichlorvos, two of the most toxic pesticides known, even more toxic than the banned DDT. They spray these poisons into cracks, crevices, drawers, damp spaces and for some species even into attics and crawl spaces. Exterminators treat for ants in a similar manner except when there are colonies under a foundation. When the house is built on a slab, it is sometimes necessary to treat sub-slab heating ducts with residual insecticides and even to soak the soil underneath the slab after drilling through it. In basements, insecticide must be injected into the walls. When there is a crawl space, colonies can be sprayed directly. Killing fleas can require complete dusting or spraying of the premises, both indoors and outdoors.

While treatments are for ants and roaches most often, termites are the most talked about pest in real estate transactions. They account for about 25 percent of the exterminating industry's revenues. Treating for termites involves some of the heaviest domestic applications of pestcides. A pest control textbook prepared by Purdue University recommends applications of one gallon of insecticide per ten square feet of foundation area. Termite treatment for a one-story home with 2,000 square feet requires an incredible 200 gallons of insecticide. Treatments are most often done right before a home changes hands, so levels are highest when a new owner moves in.

Other insecticide treatments involve spraying walls and the soil around the perimeter of a home. In addition, homeowners commonly treat for rodents and spray herbicides and fungicides to kill weeds and help maintain lawns, gardens and other vegetation. While pesticides generally deteriorate with time, high levels after treatment pose a health threat.

Health Effects of Pesticides

Despite their short-term toxicity and long-term effects, there has been little scientific work to characterize the health risks individual pesticides pose when used in the home. A recent study of environmental health risks in New England placed pesticide residues on food in the second most serious risk category, along with contaminated drinking water and indoor air pollution. However, the study did not address domestic pesticide use, even though the National Academy of Sciences has found that it is a primary source of exposure.

"Pesticides" is the generic term for functional categories of poison. The major categories are insecticides, herbicides, rodenticides and fungicides, respectively used to kill insects, weeds, rodents and fungi. In a recent study, *Consumer Reports* identified at least 80 active pesticide ingredients used domestically. Before active ingredients are applied, the manufacturer must mix them with other chemicals to form either liquid, pellets or powder. Pellets generally are used to kill rodents, for instance, and powders and liquids to kill insects. Some of the mixing ingredients themselves are toxic. People are exposed through inhalation of pesticide fumes or dust, skin absorption or ingestion.

All pesticides are toxic, since they are intended to kill a variety of life forms. In humans, many have been implicated as skin, eye and respiratory irritants and as inhibitors of the flow of energy through the nervous system. In sufficient doses, they can kill people. Many also have the potential to cause cancer, birth defects, sterility, low birth weights, genetic mutations and neurobehavioral abnormalities.

When pesticides originally were used, environmental scientists believed they degraded into harmless substances in the environment. Subsequent studies have shown that many pesticides persist or break down into substances that are even more harmful. The classic example is DDT. Field studies showed that up to 39 percent of the chemical persists in soil 17 years after being sprayed. An EPA study found that up to 50 percent of chlordane remains

10 years after being applied.

The same study said a review of scientific literature on the persistence of pesticides "leads to the disturbing conclusion that, in effect, very little is known about what happens to pesticides in the environment after application. . . . It is surprising as well as deplorable that so few scientists in this area have ventured into studying what really happens in the field."

Moreover, inadequate testing of pesticides led *Consumer Reports* to conclude in 1987 that there is a dearth of information about the safety of the 50 active pesticide ingredients used most often at home. The group found inadequate testing of 33 as a cause of cancer, 36 as a cause of mutations, 31 as a cause of birth defects, 32 as a cause of sterility, and 49 as a cause of nervous system and behavioral problems. At least one of the 50, 2,4-D, used in a wide variety of lawn and garden weed control products, has been closely linked to lymph cancer among farmers in Kansas.

The most studied household pesticide is chlordane. In 1982, the National Academy of Sciences established 5 micrograms per cubic meter of air as the safe level. Constant exposure to higher levels increases the chance of neurological disorders and chlordane is a suspected cause of cancer and birth defects.

Safe levels have not been established for the other commonly used household pesticides. For instance, chlorpyrifos is one of the chief pesticides used to kill termites now that chlordane has been taken off the market and EPA does not know if it causes cancer, mutations or is toxic to the nervous system. To correct this situation, Congress in 1988 amended the federal pesticides law to require that EPA conduct full safety evaluations over the next nine years of the 600 active pesticide ingredients used in the U.S. Meanwhile, home buyers or owners have no way of fully knowing about the safety and health effects of the many pesticides that have been and will be applied in their yards and homes. Here is a synopsis of what EPA knows about the top 10 household pesticides named by the U.S. General Accounting Office in 1986:

Captan: A fungicide used on gardens and house plants since 1951 marketed under the brand names Merpan, Orthocide, SR-406 and Vancide 89 (Note: you can identify whether an off-the-shelve product has this or any other pesticide by looking on the label for the name of the pesticide itself or any brand names listed here.) It is also used in anti-fungal shampoos, where it may pose a cancer risk of one in 10,000. EPA says animal studies show it causes cancer, mutations and reproductive problems. Neurotoxicity is unknown. It also irritates the eyes and skin.

Carbaryl: An insecticide used since 1958 on gardens, lawns, pets and homes under the brand names Sevin, Denapon, Tricarnam, and others. Animal tests show it causes mutations, but EPA does not have enough data to know if has other health effects, although it does inhibit the nervous system and in large doses damages the kidneys.

Chlordane: An insecticide used since 1948 primarily to control termites in homes and buildings under the brand names Velsicol 1068, Chlortox, Chlor-Kil, and others. Animal tests show it causes cancer and mutations and EPA believes it causes chronic liver toxicity. Other effects are unknown. In 1987 it was withdrawn from the market.

Chlorpyrifos: An insecticide used since 1965 to kill household roaches, termites, ants and other insects on lawns, shrubs and pets under the brand names Dursban, Lorsban, Pyrinex, Dowco 179, and others. It is not considered to cause birth defects or reproductive problems, but there is insufficient evidence to judge whether it is carcinogenic, mutagenic or neurotoxic, although it does inhibit the nervous system.

Diazanon: An insecticide used since 1952 to kill a variety of bugs in homes and on lawns and ornamental plants under the brand names Spectracide, Alfa-tox and others. EPA does not consider it to cause cancer or birth defects, but there are insufficient data on whether it can cause mutations, reproductive problems or neurotoxicity. It is considered a nervous system inhibitor and an eye and skin irritant.

Malathion: An insecticide used since the 1950's to kill household insects and bugs on both indoor and outdoor plants and pets. Products containing the pesticide will bear its name. EPA considers it a nervous system inhibitor, but does not have information on other possible health effects.

Maneb: A fungicide used on plants and vegetable gardens. Products will bear its name on the label. EPA believes it may affect the thyroid gland, but little else is known about its health effects.

Methoxychlor: An insecticide used in homes and on gardens and pets under Pyrocide and other brand names. It is considered an eye and skin irritant, but little else is known.

Simazine: An herbicide used since 1957 mostly to kill algae in fish ponds, swimming pools, and aquaria and to kill weeds in berry patches and orchards under the brand names Algae-A-Way, Algicide, Aquazine, and others. It is a moderate eye and skin irritant, but little else is known about it.

2-4-D: An herbicide used since 1948 as a weed killer on lawns and gardens. It is considered a reproductive toxic, an eye, skin, and respiratory irritant, and may harm the liver, kidneys, and muscles. While it has been linked to lymph cancer among farmers in Kansas, there is still considerable uncertainty regarding its potential to cause cancer and other illnesses.

How to Check for Pesticides

As a home owner or prospective buyer, it may worthwhile to check chlordane levels given the pesticide's health effects and the cost of decontamination. EPA advises you to check if your home has been treated in the last few years and:

• Family members consistently have **symptoms of pesticide exposure;**

• There are major structural flaws, like large **cracks in the foundation** or basement near where soil has been treated;

• Your basement consistently **leaks water;**

• You smell **chemical odors**, particularly when the heating or cooling system is running; and

• Immediately after treatment there are **puddles** or **stains** in your home, possibly indicating a spill during application. (While chlordane is no longer used, these signs indicate potential trouble even when substitute pesticides are used on **termites.**)

If you are buying a home, you should ask the seller when the last termite treatment was done and check for telltale signs by running the heating and cooling system to detect chemical odors and performing a thorough visual inspection.

Since the main route of chlordane exposure is through the air, it is necessary to have air samples taken. EPA recommends you select a laboratory testing firm that has experience in both indoor air sampling and pesticide analysis. You can obtain a list of firms from EPA's National Pesticide Telecommunications Network at 1 (800) 858-7378. Depending on the size of your home and the number of samples required, the cost of checking for chlordane can be $500 or more.

When you call firms, you should ask how long they

have been testing homes for chlordane and find out how they test. To get an accurate result, the firm should follow EPA test procedures outlined in the "EPA Manual of Analytical Methods for the Analysis of Pesticides in Human and Environmental Samples." Ask the contractor to show you the section of this manual that covers chlordane testing to help you understand how the test will be done. If the firm is hesitant, try another.

The test for chlordane employs a pump that draws air through a filter. EPA recommends running the pump for a substantial period of time. In the lab, the filters are then cut up and the chlordane is chemically extracted. The amount of chlordane is then compared with the volume of air pumped through the filter. The National Academy of Sciences recommends that concentrations of chlordane and other pesticides used to kill termites not exceed 5 micrograms per cubic meter of air.

Other pesticides commonly used to kill termites were heptachlor, aldrin and dieldrin, all in the chlordane family. Heptachlor was covered under the 1987 chlordane agreement, so is no longer used. Aldrin and dieldrin have not been used since 1985. In any chlordane check, make sure the testing firm looks for all of the chlordane family pesticides, since many termite treatments historically were done with mixtures of these chemicals. Today, chlorpyrifos and permethrin are the primary substitutes for chlordane.

While testing can turn up a problem with chlordane, it will not address other pesticides commonly used around the home. And although tests for other pesticides are available, they may be financially prohibitive. Therefore, the best way to protect yourself against other pesticides as a home buyer is simply to ask the seller about the history of pesticide usage and look for stored pesticides on the shelves. Geographic region is also a good indicator of likely pesticide usage.

Generally, homes in the Southeast are most likely to have been treated by commercial pesticide exterminators for pests, including termites. The accompanying map shows the percentage of homes that have been treated by commercial exterminators for pests in general, including termites, and the percentage that have been treated for termites in the ten federal regions. It should be noted that not all treatments by exterminators were for termites because many people have treated their own homes. In region IV, for instance, 44.2 percent of the homes have been treated by commercial exterminators for pests, including termites, and 54.5 percent have been treated for termites. Since not all commercial treatments were for termites, more than 54.5 percent of the homes have actually been heavily treated for pests. On the other hand, treatment rates are comparatively low in regions V and VIII.

Figure 6-1

Regional Use of Pesticides

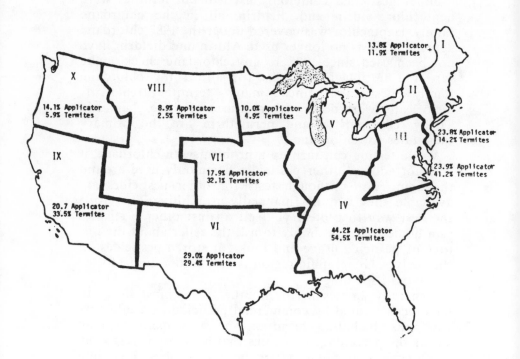

How to Prevent Pesticide Poisoning

EPA has found that chlordane levels generally are highest in basements, but can also be high in homes with crawl spaces or air ducts that run under a slab foundation. If chlordane levels are high, you probably can lower them by:

● **Sealing areas** of the home that directly contact treated soil with grout, caulk or other sealant and filling cracks in basement and ground floors and walls, joints between floors and walls, and openings around pipes, drains, and sumps;

● **Increasing the circulation of fresh air** by opening the windows and doors and using fans to mix the air;

● **Venting crawl spaces** to the outside by clearing existing vents, adding new vents, or installing a fan to draw air out;

● **Bringing air from the outside** to appliances, such as clothes dryers and furnaces, to prevent them from using inside air and in effect drawing chlordane vapors from the soil in through the cracks in your foundation; and

● **Sealing** any **openings** or joints in basement and crawl space air ducts with duct tape.

Also discard or wash any household items—such as carpets, carpet pad or curtains—that may have become coated with chlordane vapor from the air. You should wash these items several times with detergent.

These steps should acceptably lower chlordane levels that are slightly over the 5 microgram guideline. However, in cases where levels are substantially above it, structural modifications may be needed, including:

● **Replacing** or relocating air **ducts;**

● **Replacing furnace** and ventilation system with air

exchangers; and

• **Sealing crawl space** soil with a layer of concrete.

Before undertaking these steps seek professional advice. After the job is complete have your home checked again for chlordane to make sure the corrective steps have worked as promised. If chlordane levels are two or three times the 5 microgram guideline in a house you want to purchase, negotiate corrective action or find another home.

To protect yourself against exposure to other pestcides, make sure to thoroughly scrub and clean any home you are moving into, including cupboards and drawers. Dispose of any pesticide containers on the premises after consulting your local sanitation department for advice.

When using pesticides, follow the label instructions, avoid inhaling them and shower and wash your clothes afterwards. Store pesticides in their original containers with the labels attached under lock and key, preferably in an outdoor shed or cabinet. At all costs, keep them away from children. If someone in your family swallows a pesticide, follow the first aid treatment on the label. Then go to the hospital or doctor immediately with the label.

Following these steps will help protect you and your family from the dangers of pesticides used around the home.

CHECKLIST FOR PESTICIDES

Checking For Pesticides:

☐ Are there chemical odors indoors, particularly when the air conditioning or heating is running?

☐ Ask the home seller about pesticide usage.

☐ Are pesticides stored in the home?

☐ Does anyone have symptoms of pesticide poisoning?

☐ Is the home in a region of the country where pesticides are heavily used?

Selecting A Chlordane Test Firm:

☐ Obtain a list of firms from EPA at 1 (800) 858-7378.

☐ Make sure firm is familiar with EPA procedures.

☐ Make sure firm has experience both in pesticides and indoor air monitoring.

☐ Clarify that all chlordane family pesticides will be measured.

☐ Obtain competitive bids.

Solving a Chlordane Problem:

☐ Seal and fill possible vapor entry points around foundation and walls.

☐ Increase ventilation.

☐ Bring outside air to dryer and furnace.

☐ Vent crawl spaces.

☐ Seal joints and openings on basement and crawl space air ducts.

☐ Inquire about structural improvements if chlordane levels are high.

Other Tips:

☐ Clean home before moving in.

☐ Store pesticides outside in original, labeled containers.

Chapter Seven

Drinking Water

Cher Fish sat one summer day in 1988 amidst the boxes packed with her family's belongings. She had loved her mountain home, high above polluted Los Angeles. It stood on a ridge overlooking Lake Arrowhead, filled with clear blue water fed by mountain springs. But Fish and family had to leave. One day in February things went awry in their pristine mountain community when Fish turned on her kitchen faucet and gasoline poured out. The family stopped drinking the water immediately, but Fish and her infant daughter developed rashes from bathing.

Fish was not alone in her plight. Leaking underground gasoline storage tanks had tainted well water for 720 homes in the Lake Arrowhead Villas development. Ironically, the leaky tanks were owned by the small water company that served the community and were located just 50 feet from the firm's two wells.

Fish recalled being told by the company that her home was supplied by pure well water. "I really trusted people, trusted the system so I let my little girl drink that water. I made her food with it," she told the *Los Angeles Times*, which reported her story. Now a skeptic, however, Fish said the first thing she would do in her new home is test the water.

You too should be concerned enough about your tap water to find out what contaminants are in it and install a purification system in your home if contaminant levels are high. And if you already own or are buying a home with a private well, you should make sure it is soundly constructed and will not pose problems.

You need to take these steps because throughout the United States and other industrialized countries, drinking water is contaminated with trace levels of chemical contaminants. Chemicals are used on such a widespread basis—at the corner gas station, in the home, on the farm, and in industry—that both surface water and groundwater have become widely contaminated. The congressional Office of Technology Assessment in 1984 found more than 200 contaminants in wellwater, including many associated with cancer and other health effects. Other studies have found that a variety of chemicals pollute lakes and rivers too. In Louisiana, federal data show that 136 chemical plants dumped 774 million pounds of toxic pollutants into waterways in 1987 alone.

And the sources of surface water contamination are not restricted to chemical plants. Grease, soot, lead from gasoline, and other grime from autos wash off the roads each time it rains into streams, rivers and lakes. Household and agricultural pesticides trickle into surface water. In Kansas City, for instance, public health officials have closed a section of the Blue River to fishing due to contamination with the pesticide chlordane. The pesticide, used for years to kill termites, washes into the river from Kansas City homes each time it rains. Wastewater from sewage treatment plants and industrial facilities enters rivers and lakes around the clock. Even though it has been treated, it is far from pure. And in backyards across America, seepage from septic tanks in unsewered areas pollutes streams and lakes.

Likewise, contaminants percolate into groundwater from a multitude of sources—underground gasoline tanks, hazardous waste dumps, municipal garbage dumps, septic tanks, roadways and farm fields and yards sprayed with pesticides and fertilizer to name but a few. A National Academy of Sciences study of Long Island, where three million people rely solely on groundwater, found that:

• Some 5,200 tons of nitrate contamination a year percolates into the island's groundwater from use of lawn fertilizer;

• Almost 70,000 gallons of septic tank cleaning solvents enter Nassau County's groundwater each year; and

• Numerous wells are tainted with a variety of pesticides, which are used on farms, yards, parks and golf courses.

While massive efforts under way to clean up and prevent contamination, the chemical poisoning of drinking water is likely to remain a problem well into the 21st century. Moreover, environmental officials' increased ability to measure and track drinking water quality has shown that mineral, bacterial and viral contamination remain a problem, particularly in homes with backyard wells or served by small community wells.

Yet there is little reason to despair and see the problem as too massive to cope with individually. Indeed, home-based water purification systems are readily available. And those with backyard septic tanks and wells can benefit from state of the art knowledge about how to prevent and solve water contamination problems.

Water Sanitation

Fortunately, water is a renewable resource. Rainwater is relatively pure and constantly refreshes waterways and groundwater. However, at once a body of water and the land rainwater passes over is polluted, the pollution tends to linger. Indeed, before passage of environmental laws, human waste and industrial pollution literally killed some bodies of water, rendering them unusable for drinking, fishing or recreation. Cleveland's Cuyahoga River, which caught fire, became a symbol of the ills of water pollution and galvanized cleanup efforts.

While the waterways are cleaner, toxic contamination remains largely unaddressed. And toxic contamination of groundwater, including backyard wells, has just recently come into focus.

To protect yourself and family from contamination, it is helpful to have a basic understanding of water sanitation, an ancient art that most people in the industrialized world take for granted. In its simplest form, it involves isolating human waste—a medium for dysentery, infectious hepatitis, typhoid and other diseases—from drinking water. Today, sanitation has become more complex, encompassing water reuse and treatment for biological and chemical contaminants as increases in population and industrialization have caused water use to climb dramatically. By the time New Orleans takes its drinking water out of the Mississippi River, for instance, it has flowed through millions of people, thousands of factories and hundreds of sewer systems. Understandably, New Orleans is not reknown for high quality drinking water. Groundwater in the area is even more contaminated than the river.

Yet there are no outbreaks of waterborne diseases in New Orleans, because the human waste is removed in each community upstream before the water is discharged. And as an added safeguard, the water is treated in downstream communities before being used for drinking water. So as a resident of a community served by a metropolitan sewer and drinking water system, while you should be concerned with chemical contaminants, you have little to worry about when it comes to waterborne diseases. However, if you live in or are buying one of the almost 20 million U.S. homes that have a private well and septic tank or cess pool, you are responsible for your own sanitation, namely to ensure that your waste will not:

● Contaminate drinking water;

● Create a public health hazard by being accessible to insects, rodents or other carriers that can come into contact with food or drinking water;

● Be accessible to children;

● Violate laws or regulations governing water pollution;

• Pollute waters of any bathing beach, shellfish breeding ground, or waterway used for recreation; or

• Give rise to a nuisance, due to odor or unsightly appearance.

To ensure proper sanitation, you must make sure that your home wastewater system adequately decomposes human waste and that the water ultimately passed through it is clarified, that is, substantially free of solid organic waste. You also must be sure that the effluent does not carry chemicals that can contaminate your own well or that of a neighbor. Finally, you must make sure your well is not contaminated and is placed and constructed in a manner that eliminates the possibility of contamination.

If you are connected to one of the 40,000 small centralized systems that serve fewer than 500 people, you also may want to find out where the well or water supply is located. Some of these small systems have a history of frequently violating basic sanitation standards.

If you are served by a large centralized water system, chemical contaminants should be a concern. While the system operator is responsible for meeting drinking water standards, safe levels have not been set for a number of contaminants. Moreover, it remains to be seen how these standards, only mandated by Congress in 1986, will ultimately be enforced. Because of this, you should consider installing a drinking water treatment system in your home. It would be better if drinking water had been protected at the source, but it has not been in too many cases. Consequently, removing contaminants is the only way to protect your health.

Here then is a guide to protecting yourself against drinking water contamination in the home, including information on known contaminants, their health effects, and safe levels.

Health Effects

Drinking water contaminants can broadly be divided into five categories:

• **Inorganic minerals** and metals, which occur naturally or are introduced by human activity;

• **Radioactive substances**, which generally occur naturally;

• Viruses, bacterial, and other **microbiological contaminants** that are introduced by human and animal waste;

• **Volatile organic chemicals**—which are prone to evaporation—from paints, gasoline and industrial chemicals and solvents; and

• **Organic chemicals**, which include pesticides and industrial chemicals that do not evaporate.

There are several contaminants in each category and the federal Environmental Protection Agency is setting standards for each. EPA's task is to determine what level of each contaminant will not result in adverse health effects and then determine the treatment method that will come closest to this level. In many cases, EPA considers only the complete absence of a contaminant safe, yet there is no known treatment that can completely remove the contaminant. In other cases the safe level is technologically attainable. In either case, EPA must set two standards for each contaminant: a safe level and a technologically-feasible level. In addition, the agency sets standards to prevent what it considers cosmetic health effects. Microbiological contaminants cause acute diseases, such as dysentary. Between 1971 and 1981, some 82,000 cases of such waterborne diseases were reported to the Centers for Disease Control. Outbreaks of giardia lamblia traced to animal waste have been known to kill some victims.

Inorganic contaminants can cause a variety of acute

and long-term diseases. Too much fluoride, for instance, mottles the teeth and eventually causes a crippling bone disease. High levels of nitrate have been known to cause "blue-baby syndrome," in which infants' blood loses the capacity to carry sufficient oxygen. The syndrome can cause brain damage and even death.

Radioactive substances have been associated with cancer, birth defects and sterility. Naturally-occuring radon, for instance, causes lung cancer. Water drawn from wells carries radon into the house where it is released into the air and breathed.

Volatile organic compounds have been associated with cancer, leukemia, and other killing diseases. Benzene, a component of gasoline, is a known carcinogen. Trichloroethylene, a solvent used in dry cleaning and industry, is a suspected cause of liver cancer.

Organic chemicals have also been linked with cancer. For instance, ethylene dibromide, a pesticide used for years before it was found to migrate into groundwater, is a suspected cause of cancer. Trihalomethanes, a class of organic chemicals, are produced within drinking water pipes when chlorine used to disinfect drinking water reacts with organic matter. These contaminants are common in large, centrally-operated drinking water systems. At least one of them, chloroform, is known to cause kidney damage and is suspected of causing cancer.

EPA's Limits on Contaminants

Below are EPA's technologically-feasible limits for drinking water contaminants. In most cases EPA has set specific numerical values. For microbiological contaminants, it has established acceptable treatment methods, which are discussed briefly below.

Limits for Contaminants

Contaminant	Level
Inorganics:	
Arsenic	0.05 mg/l
Barium	1 mg/l
Cadmium	0.01 mg/l
Chromium	0.05 mg/l
Fluoride	4 mg/l
Lead	0.05 mg/l
Mercury	0.002 mg/l
Nitrate	10 mg/l
Selenium	0.01 mg/l
Silver	0.05 mg/l
Organics:	
Endrin	0.0002 mg/l
Lindane	0.004 mg/l
Methoxychlor	0.1 mg/l
Toxaphene	0.005 mg/l
Chlorophenoxys	0.1 mg/l
Total Trihalomethanes	0.1 mg/l
Volatile Organics:	
Trichloroethylene	0.005 ppm
Carbon Tetrachloride	0.005 ppm
1,2-Dichloroethane	0.005 ppm
Vinyl Chloride	0.002 ppm
Benzene	0.005 ppm
1,1-Dichloroethylene	0.007 ppm
Para-dichlorobenzene	0.075 ppm
1,1,1-Trichloroethane	0.2 ppm
Radioactive Substances:	
Radium-226 & 228	5 picocuries/liter
Gross Alpha Particles	15 pCi/l
Total Radioactivity	4 millirem dose/year

To control microbilogical contaminants, EPA generally has prescribed that surface water be filtered through sand and disinfected and that groundwater be disinfected. However, this is only in cases where sampling indicates a contamination problem.

Home Treatment for Chemicals

The only way to truly determine if your tap water is chemically tainted is to analyze it. If your water comes from a centralized drinking water system that serves more than 25 people, it is the responsibility of the operator to analyze regularly for contaminants and make the data available to you. If you own or are buying a home with a private well, you should ask for any groundwater analysis data available from public health or drinking water authorities. If data are not available, have your water analyzed. Check with EPA's drinking water hotline (800) 426-4791 or your state drinking water authority for recommendations on laboratories and what contaminants to test for, since not all areas have the same problems. Some states may provide analysis for free or at minimal charge. Otherwise, you can expect to pay around $1,000 to test for the full range of contaminants.

If chemical contaminants exceed EPA standards, or if you are worried about contamination nevertheless, there are a variety of home treatment systems you can install. They range from faucet attachments to whole-house systems. Bear in mind that the primary task is to purify drinking water, not water used on the lawn or to wash the car, flush the toilet or launder the clothes. Exposure in these uses is minimal. A good system under the kitchen sink may be most appropriate.

Consumer's Reports magazine reports there are 10 million U.S. homes already equipped with water purifiers and 400 companies that make treatment systems. Systems are available at hardware stores and from vendors listed in the *Yellow Pages*. These are the four primary technologies used in home water treatment:

Water Softening or ion exchange: This technique uses sodium or potassium chloride pellets to remove calcium, magnesium, some toxic metals, and radioactive radium through a process known as cation exchange. There are some models which employ anion exchange to remove nitrates.

Activated Carbon: This technique uses a carbon filter that tends to do a good job of extracting volatile organic chemicals and many organic chemicals. Make sure you change the carbon frequently to prevent buildup of chemicals and also bacteria, since it is a good medium for bacterial growth.

Reverse Osmosis: This technique uses a membrane with holes that are so small only water, for the most part, can pass through. Particle contaminants and other large molecules are literally left behind.

Distillation: In this technique, water is boiled in one container and condensed in a separate clean one. Minerals and other solids are left behind. Activated carbon is needed to remove liquid organics. Distillation systems must be cleaned frequently and generally can produce only small quantities of drinking water.

In addition, you can purchase an activiated alumina system to reduce levels of fluoride. Handling a lead problem is covered in Chapter Five. To eliminate radon, you can install an aeration device outside on the central water pipe serving your home.

Whole-house and reverse osmosis systems can cost up to $1,000, plus installation. Filter media have to be replaced, which is an additional cost. In some cases you may need two or three systems to do an adequate job.

While home purifiers reduce contaminant levels, they do not totally eliminate contaminants. Moreover, their effectiveness varies, depending on design, maintenance, the concentration of contaminants, and other factors. So when purchasing a system, know what contaminants you need to treat and read the product literature to see how efficiently a system will remove those contaminants. Also, look for the seals of the Water Quality Association, a trade group composed of firms that manufacture home purification systems, and the National Sanitation Foundation, a non-profit testing and standard-setting organization. Both have standards for home treatment devices. Finally, install your system properly and follow the manufacturers maintenance instructions.

Wells

If you are buying or already own a home with a well, you should make sure it will not pose sanitary or chemical contamination problems. A sanitary engineer or inspector should be consulted. Homes with private wells or in subdivisions served by community wells are particularly prone to sanitation problems, since they generally have septic tanks. Their wells are also prone to chemical contamination, since they are most often shallow and tap unconfined aquifers.

Wells are drilled to draw groundwater, which is found in layers of the earth known as aquifers. Deep aquifers generally are free from man-made contaminants, especially if they are confined, that is, covered with an impermeable layer of clay or rock through which water will not seep. Groundwater in unconfined aquifers or near the earth in alluvial soil, typical of river valleys and flood plains, is prone to contamination since chemicals from the earth's surface—such as pesticides or gasoline—percolate down with rain.

Another factor is that groundwater moves. If your neighbor's land is contaminated and is uphill, or upgradient in geological parlance, your groundwater can become contaminated. Plumes of contamination from hazardous waste sites or farm fields sprayed with pesticides have been known to travel for miles.

To make sure your well is free of biological contaminants, have it tested by a qualified laboratory. To find out if your well may be chemically contaminated, check with local or state health and drinking water authorities. They may have test information and can give advice on treatment techniques. If not, you may need to have a laboratory perform tests. If chemical contaminants exceed EPA standards, drink bottled water until you can install an adequate treatment system. To protect yourself against future contamination problems:

• **Do not use pesticides** or an overabundance of fertilizer on your land;

• **Make sure your well is upgradient** and laterally at least 50 feet from any septic tank, 100 feet from any cesspool and 75 feet from any privy;

• **Make sure your well is grouted** to prevent contaminants from draining down through a crack or space between dirt and the outside of the well casing; and

• Make sure **abandoned wells** on your property or nearby **are adequately sealed** to prevent contaminants from entering groundwater.

Pumping water from wells creates a cone of depression in the aquifer. Water is actually drawn from a 360 degree area around the well, both upgradient and downgradient. Because of this, it is important to make sure there is adequate lateral separation between your well and any downgradient source of contamination, such as a septic tank or cesspool. Therefore, the distances recommended here for lateral separation are absolute minimums. Greater separation is preferable. Animal feedlots, and the attendant manure, can pose a hazard too.

In coastal areas, seawater can be drawn into a freshwater aquifer, particularly if the aquifer is heavily used or the year has been unusually dry. This phenomenon, known as saltwater intrusion, has ruined many a well.

Finally, EPA has estimated that there may be more underground gasoline or fuel oil tanks at homes on farms and rural communities than at gasoline stations. So if you are buying a rural home, make sure to find out if there is an in-use or abandoned tank. Have the wellwater tested and the tank checked for leaks. If the water is contaminated or the tank has leaked, you probably had better find another home to buy. Cleaning up leaky tanks can easily cost $100,000, even more. If you own a home with a private gasoline tank, at a minimum test it for leaks with a dip stick. Better yet, have automated leak detection and cathodic corrosion protection systems installed. Cathodic protection employs a weak electrical current to prevent the steel tank rusting. At any rate, consult your state environmental agency for advice if you have a tank (See Appendix).

Septic Tanks

Proper placement, construction and maintenance of septic tanks is an integral part of ensuring sanitation in your home water system. Septic tanks are a leading cause of groundwater contamination, fouling aquifers with bacteria from human waste, chemicals flushed down the drain, and nitrate, a byproduct when human waste decomposes. The congressional Office of Technology Assessment estimates that 820 billion gallons of household sewage a year flows through some 20 million septic tanks, cesspools, and other home-based wastewater systems in the United States.

Septic tanks are designed to trap and decompose the solid organic waste from households and to discharge the wastewater to the ground. They do not adequately remove bacteria from the wastewater, but the bacteria are trapped and eventually die in the soil into which the wastewater is discharged. The main function of a septic tank is to keep the solid material from clogging the wastewater disposal field that lies beyond it. The system must be able to accommodate the 45 gallons of wastewater a day that each person in your household will produce.

In a septic tank, the water is slowed to allow solid materials to settle. Bacteria that live without oxygen decompose this material into a sludge that settles to the bottom of the tank and a scum that floats on top of the water. A baffle separates the floating layer of scum from the outlet pipe where the wastewater is discharged into perforated pipes that run underground through a drainage field and gradually allow the water to percolate downward. The soil must be porous enough to allow the wastewater to percolate down and not ever rise to the surface of the earth. If solid material is allowed to leave the septic tank, it will eventually clog the drainage field and create a backup of sewage to the yard and house above.

If you are buying a home with a septic tank, have the home water and wastewater system checked by a sanitary engineer. And if you have a home with a septic tank, make sure to have it inspected and pumped out by a certified septic tank service firm at least once a year. This firm should never disinfect a tank after pumping it because this will destroy the colony of anerobic bacteria that decomposes the solid waste.

Other considerations are to:

• Use household cleansers and detergents moderately since they will wind up in your groundwater;

• Avoid putting any paint, solvents, or other chemicals down your drain, including septic tank cleaning solvents;

• Flush a small amount of bleach down the drain if you smell septic tank odors;

• Avoid flushing any paper but toilet paper into the tank; and

• Post a chart in the garage giving the location and instructions on inspection and maintenance of the septic tank.

Remember that a septic tank generally will provide only 20 to 40 years of service. So if you are buying a home, find out how old tank is and plan for its eventual replacement.

Whether you live in the city and are served by a water utility or in a rural area with your own water system, you are now prepared to protect yourself and family against chemical and bacterial contamination of drinking water.

CHECKLIST FOR WATER

If Served By A Central Water System:

□ Ask the operator for water analysis data.

□ Compare the data to EPA standards.

□ If levels are higher, install home water purifier.

□ If levels worry you, install purification equipment.

If The House Has A Well:

□ Make sure it is uphill from septic tank or cesspool.

□ Make sure space between dirt and well casing is grouted.

□ Have water analyzed for contaminants.

□ If contaminants exceed EPA standards, discuss with local health authorities and install appropriate home treatment system.

If The House Has A Septic Tank

□ Make sure it is downhill from any well and at least 50 feet away.

□ Have it regularly inspected and pumped.

Before buying, check the soundness of any underground tank.

Chapter Eight

Hazardous Chemicals

in the Neighborhood

It was a still, hot night in Los Angeles as residents in several suburban communities slumbered. But shortly after 3 a.m. on Saturday, Sept. 3, 1988, thousands awoke to the blare of a voice over a loudspeaker warning them to evacuate immediately. The Parazan family in East Los Angeles thought it was just a radio blasting from a car full of teenagers cruising by. But when they smelled chlorine, they realized they had to leave.

The family joined up to 27,000 people who fled a five-square-mile area in the communities of Commerce, East Los Angeles, Montebello, and Monterey Park. They spent the remainder of the night and morning camped out with blankets on high school baseball fields and at other impromptu shelters set up by the American Red Cross, said the Los Angeles Times, which reported the incident.

Authorities ordered the widespread evacuation after a powder used to make chlorine pool tablets at a plant owned by the Grow Group Inc. reacted with moisture in the air and ignited. The powder, stored in cardboard barrels, produced a variety of toxic chlorine gases. The toxic cloud hung in the still air over the evacuated area for hours, causing at least 68 people to seek treatment for respiratory problems.

Workers on the grave-yard shift at a nearby paper plant ran to an all-night restaurant for cover, but the toxic cloud eventually overcame them in the eatery. Seven were hospitalized for nausea, chest pain, and breathing problems. It was the third time in 1988 alone workers at the plant had to flee toxic clouds.

Public health authorities said after an investigation the Grow Group had been storing the powder improperly and charged the firm with violating environmental regulations. A separate inquiry by elected officials into the firm's history revealed that the alleged improper storage was detected long before the September incident. Indeed, there even had been an earlier, smaller chlorine cloud at the plant. However, environmental agencies never followed up due to a shortage of inspectors.

The Grow Group incident typifies sudden toxic releases that occur almost daily across the country. There simply are not enough environmental inspectors, nor will there ever be, to ensure that chemical accidents do not occur. Moreover, aside from accidental releases, a recent Congressional report documented that industries routinely release 2.4 billion pounds of toxic air pollutants in American communities each year. In cities, suburbs, and towns across the nation, plants that store, use, and release toxics are side-by-side with housing, schools, nursing homes and hospitals.

In addition, there are thousands of hazardous waste sites in the U.S., according to the Environmental Protection Agency, a countless number of which abut back yards and neighborhoods. These sites eventually will be cleaned up, but some of the restoration methods, such as incinerating contaminated soil, may present problems for those nearby.

Sanitary landfills used to bury some 250 million tons of garbage produced in the U.S. each year regularly plague nearby neighborhoods with foul odors. Moreover, in crowded urban areas developers build homes atop closed landfills, which are prone to subsidence and continue to belch methane, vinyl chloride, and other gases for years as buried refuse decays. Sewage treatment plants are prone to producing odors that create a public nuisance in surrounding neighborhoods and are a major source of toxic air pollution, particularly in cities where industries dump waste water down the drain.

Fortunately, as a potential home buyer you can obtain information about the location of hazardous waste sites and facilities where toxics are used and released. In amending the Superfund law in 1986, Congress added little known provisions that require about 4.5 million facilities nationwide to report on the toxic chemicals they use and release routinely and accidentally. The provisions, known as Title III of Superfund, or the Emergency Planning and Community Right-to-Know Act, further require authorities who receive the data to make it publicly available. Local authorities must prepare community evacuation and response plans in the event of a toxic release.

How to Find Out the Chemicals in Your Neighborhood

Under Title III, you have the right to find out what chemicals are stored, used, and released, both routinely and accidentally, from most sizable facilities. You also have the right to review a standard form, known as a material safety data sheet, that tells what is known about the properties and health effects of a chemical. Finally, you have the right to both find out about your community's chemical emergency response plan and participate in developing and updating that plan. Congress intended Title III to empower you to protect yourself and family and gain information you can use to make your community a safer and healthier place to live.

Title III calls for each state to have an emergency response commission and each community to have an emergency planning committee. All data under Title III are publicly available from your local committee. Often, you can find out how to get data by contacting your local fire department. When seeking data, have as much information as possible about a facility, at a minimum the correct name and the city. An exact street address is preferable. Your state commission also can provide all data reported under Title III, except for your local emergency response plan, which is available only from your local committee. Here are the telephone numbers of the state commissions, which can refer you to your local committee:

Alabama	(205) 834-1375	Montana	(406) 444-3111
	(205) 271-7700	Nebraska	(402) 471-4230
Alaska	(907) 465-2600	Nevada	(702) 885-5375
Arizona	(602) 244-0504	New Hamp.	(603) 271-2231
Arkansas	(501) 562-7444	New Jersey	(609) 882-2000
California	(916) 427-4201		(609) 292-6714
Colorado	(303) 273-1622	New Mexico	(505) 827-3375
	(303) 331-4600	New York	(518) 457-2222
Connecticut	(203) 566-4856	No. Carolina	(919) 733-3867
Delaware	(302) 736-4321	No. Dakota	(701) 224-2348
D.C.	(207) 727-6161		(701) 224-2111
Florida	(904) 488-1900	Ohio	(614) 644-2260
Georgia	(404) 656-3500	Oklahoma	(405) 521-2481
Guam	(671) 477-9841	Oregon	(503) 378-3473
Hawaii	(808) 548-5832	Pennsylvania	(717) 783-8150
Idaho	(208) 342-0031	Puerto Rico	(809) 725-5140
Illinois	(217) 782-2700		(809) 722-1175
Indiana	(317) 243-5176	Rhode Island	(401) 421-7333
Iowa	(515) 281-6175	So. Carolina	(803) 734-0442
Kansas	(913) 296-1690	So. Dakota	(605) 773-3153
Kentucky	(502) 564-8680	Tennessee	(615) 252-3300
Louisiana	(504) 925-6113	Texas	(512) 465-2138
Maine	(800) 452-8735	Utah	(801) 533-5271
Maryland	(301) 225-5780		(801) 538-6121
Mass.	(617) 727-7775	Vermont	(802) 828-2286
	(617) 875-1381	Virgin Is.	(809) 774-3320
	(617) 292-5810	Virginia	(804) 225-2667
Michigan	(517) 373-8481	Washington	(206) 753-2200
Minnesota	(612) 296-0481	W. Virginia	(304) 348-2755
Mississippi	(601) 960-9000	Wisconsin	(608) 266-3232
Missouri	(314) 751-7929		

When you call, tell the commission you want the following information on any facility:

- Material safety data sheets;

- Emergency procedures;

- Hazardous chemical inventory forms; and

- Toxic chemical release inventory information.

It is a good idea to be familiar with your community's emergency plan, so also be sure to get information from your local committee. You can obtain further information on this program by calling EPA's Emergency Planning and Community Right-to-Know Information Hotline between 8:30 a.m. and 7:30 p.m. Eastern time at (800) 535 -0202, or (202) 479-2449 in Washington, D.C.

Hazardous Waste Sites

Hazardous waste first gripped public attention in the late 1970's when residents of the Love Canal area near Niagara Falls, N.Y., were forced to abandon their homes when chemicals seeped into their basements. In response to the shock and growing realization that Love Canal was but one of many places around the U.S. where chemical wastes had been dumped, Congress passed the Superfund law in 1980. Superfund originally was to finance cleanups at fewer than 1,000 sites, but as environmental authorities investigated the list of sites needing attention grew. By 1984, EPA estimated cleanup would be needed at almost 380,000 sites in communities and neighborhoods across the nation. Consequently, Congress expanded Superfund in 1986.

Today, cleanups are under way. Many are as simple as removing underground storage tanks that have corroded and leaked gasoline into the soil. Others involve covering soil contaminated with metals to prevent human exposure. In some cases, cleanups simply involve drilling wells to pump and treat contaminated groundwater. Still others require removing contaminated soil and carting it away for incineration or incinerating it onsite. Many large sites involve all of these techniques, and more.

It is not easy to generalize about the health threat posed by hazardous waste sites and the cleanups themselves. Each site has different combinations and concentrations of chemicals. Each has different geological and climatic conditions that will influence exposure to toxics. And each cleanup will be somewhat unique, although the methods may be similar. In general, however, EPA recently placed hazardous waste sites in the lowest of five environmental health risk categories studied in New England.

Yet, if you are buying a home or already own one, you should take the time to find out if there are major hazardous waste sites nearby, since they have the potential to affect your health, quality of life, and property value. No matter how little health risk may be involved, discovery and cleanup of a hazardous waste site is an emotionally charged issue in most communities. Contact the state and federal environmental authorities listed on page 98 to see where there may be hazardous waste sites in your community.

Should authorities find a hazardous waste site in your community, do not expect quick cleanup action. This is because authorities must try to identify and secure financing for cleanup from the land owners and waste dumpers before expending public money for total cleanup. Securing financing from the so-called responsible parties is a complicated and long legal process.

However, do not panic because the authorities should immediately secure and stabilize the site to remove any "imminent" threat to public health. The next step will be to characterize the type and extent of contamination and outline several options for cleaning up the site. This study can take years to complete, but eventually a cleanup method is selected and work goes forward. The whole process is public and you can expect several informational meetings initially and eventually a hearing on selecting a cleanup method. You also are likely to receive brochures or flyers from authorities regarding the status of the project and find regular coverage in your local paper.

The McColl site in Fullerton, California, is a major hazardous waste now nearing cleanup. Oil refineries in the Los Angeles area used the site to dispose of waste from 1942 through 1962 when it was surrounded by an oil field to the north and a hog farm to the south. In the late 1950s, however, a golf course was built atop some of the pits used for waste disposal and in 1968 homes were built on the eastern border of the site. Eventually, homes were built all around and the unsuspecting residents soon began complaining of odors and health problems they attributed to the site.

Authorities investigated the complaints and in 1983 covered the contaminated area, which decreased the odors. In early 1989, EPA proposed excavating 6,000 truckloads of contaminated soil and incinerating it onsite, which will take four to seven years and cost $117 million. The other options are to haul the soil away to be burned or disposed of or to permanently contain the waste onsite. All the options involve several years of work and will result in the release of some contaminants into the air. In addition, the agency plans to study whether it needs to clean up groundwater, which would involve additional work and potential pollution of the air.

McColl typifies many of the 2,000 sites that eventually will be cleaned up under Superfund. It also typifies what will be done at several smaller sites being handled under state laws. As a potential home buyer you will want to know about such a site before buying a home nearby, and as a nearby resident you surely will want to keep abreast of developments there.

Other Facilities

Garbage landfills and sewage treatment plants are the source of numerous complaints from residents who live nearby, so consider this when purchasing a home.

Landfills are places where garbage is buried on a daily basis until the area is filled and then the land is frequently sold for development. A variety of materials, including household pesticides, spray cans, paints, and other materials are disposed of in landfills. Eventually these containers rot and the material inside is released. It can enter the groundwater, ooze to the surface, and be released into the air. Other material slowly rots and produces methane and hydrogen sulfide gas, which seeps up into the air. In Los Angeles, air pollution control authorities have determined that landfill gases are a major contributor to smog and are requiring that wells be installed to collect and route gases to a burner before they can enter the air. These gases can be produced for decades and are the source of many odor complaints. Dust blown from the surface of operating landfills is another source of frequent complaints.

If buying a home built on top of a landfill, check into whether there has been any problem with subsidence and foundation cracking in the neighborhood. Ask neighbors, the city building inspector, and the local newspaper about such problems. As garbage rots, the soil above it shifts.

Because landfill space is short in many areas, some cities are beginning to incinerate garbage. However, incineration can pose hazards too, such as smoke, odors, and ash, in which metals are concentrated. Unless ash is contained onsite and kept wet when being transported away for burial it can blow into your neighborhood. Incineration of plastic is known to emit trace amounts of toxic air pollutants that will increase the cancer risk of nearby residents.

Finally, sewage treatment plants are a major source of odors and toxic air pollution. A variety of toxics are flushed down the drain both in homes and industry and when the water comes into contact with the air in a sewage treatment plant many of these toxics evaporate. The solid sludge left after treating the dirty water must be dealt with. Some sewage treatment plants burn it and others compost it, another source of odors.

In general, these facilities are heavily regulated and have good pollution control equipment, but almost no facility has a perfect record. So be realistic when buying a home nearby. It is unrealistic to expect they will not be a nuisance from time to time and a source of toxic exposure. And if you do not want to subject yourself to such a nuisance, make sure to find out where these facilities are located before purchasing a home. Your city or county sanitation department can tell you.

CHECKLIST FOR NEIGHBORHOOD HAZARDS

Dangerous Chemicals in the Neighborhood:

☐ Cruise the area to identify any industries.

☐ Call your state commission for information on plants.

☐ Ask how to contact your local emergency planning committee.

☐ Familiarize yourself with your local committee's emergency response plan.

Nearby Hazardous Waste Sites:

☐ Call your EPA regional office

☐ Call your state environmental agency

☐ Ask for literature on any site, often available at a local library

Other Facilities:

☐ Call your local sanitation department for the locations of landfills, garbage incinerators and sewage treatment plants.

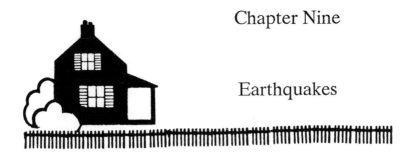

Chapter Nine

Earthquakes

Priscilla Oganesoff began the day Oct. 1, 1987, with breakfast in the dining room of her Whittier, California, home. She sat with her children John and Natalie as on any other morning, but suddenly her home began to shake. She grabbed the children and proclaimed, "It's okay. It's going to stop right now." But then the walls opened and they could see the sky. Moments later the earth stood still.

Geologists reported the earthquake registered 6.1 on the Richter Scale and was centered in Whittier. The shock waves from the quake and a severe aftershock at 3:59 a.m. on Oct. 4 caused some $200 million of damage to more than 10,000 residences and businesses in the area around Whittier, a nearby suburb of Los Angeles.

In Oganesoff's neighborhood, as reported in the Orange County Register, scores of old homes were literally knocked off their foundations. Damage was so heavy and widespread that many residents still lived in trailers six months later. Homeowners faced a shortage of skilled carpentars and repairmen, insurance problems, and paperwork hassles. In the meantime, they had to scrounge daily showers from neighbors.

In most of the U.S., earthquakes of such magnitude are unlikely to occur. However, in many areas, particularly in California, they pose a daily threat. While better construction practices in the U.S. make it highly unlikely a severe quake would cause property damage and loss of life on the scale often seen abroad, even here quakes can cause substantial damage.

Today, Whittier shows few signs of the 1987 earthquake, but residents remain braced because another could occur at any moment without warning. To protect your life and home in an earthquake area, you must be prepared. Moreover, when buying an older home, look for certain structural deficiencies that could pose trouble. If you already own a home, consider correcting any deficiencies.

Understanding Earthquakes

Geologists believe the earth's outer crust consists of pieces that float over a fluid mantle, like icebergs on the ocean. These pieces are held together by immense pressure that is released in a sudden jolt when it overcomes the force of friction. Such sudden releases trigger earthquakes where the pieces of crust meet and rub against each other, areas known as faults. In a quake, one piece of crust suddenly moves relative to the other, either laterally or vertically.

Faults exist throughout the country. But earthquakes are most notable along the junctions of major pieces of crust, known as global tectonic plates. In these zones, faults are extensive and more active. California is one area where tectonic plates grind against each other along the San Andreas fault, which is criss-crossed by countless smaller faults. Earthquakes commonly occur on the West Coast, from Alaska to San Diego, and throughout much of the West. They occasionally occur in other areas, such as New England and the Midwest.

Quakes are measured on the Richter Scale, which indicates how much energy is released. Note that the energy released progresses logarithmically as the magnitude increases.

The Power of Earthquakes

Magnitude of Quake (Richter Scale)	T.N.T. Equivalent
1	6 ounces
2	13 pounds
3	397 pounds
4	6 tons
5	199 tons
6	6,270 tons
7	199,000 tons
8	6.27 million tons
9	199 million tons

While this scale tells how much energy is released, it does not indicate how much damage can be expected. Damage is shown with the Modified Mercalli Intensity Scale. The following chart shows what to expect in earthquakes of various magnitudes.

Scales of Earthquake Damage

Richter Scale	Mercalli Scale	Damage
1	I	Not felt.
2	I-II	Generally not felt. Delicately suspended objects may swing.
3	III	Noticeably felt, but many are not recognized as an earthquake.
4	V	Felt by almost everyone; many awakened. Some dishes and windows broken; some cracked plaster; unstable objects overturned.
5	VI-VII	Felt by all; many run outside. Plaster and chimney damage occurs; considerable damage in poorly-designed structures.
6	VII-VIII	Damage considerable in ordinary structures with panel walls thrown out of frame structures, partial collapse and toppled chimneys.
7	IX-X	Many masonry and some wellbuilt wooden structures destroyed; underground pipes broken; ground badly cracked; landslides.
8	XI	Few masonry structures left; bridges destroyed.
9	XII	Damage is total.

Before the 1987 Whittier quake, the Los Angeles area experienced its last damaging quake in 1971 in suburban San Fernando Valley. That quake was 6.4 on the Richter Scale, damaged hospitals and caused a freeway bridge to collapse. Twenty-six people were killed and damage exceeded $1 billion. A 1933 earthquake in Long Beach killed 120 people. It had a magnitude of 6.3. Many others have occurred in the state and geologists for years have been predicting the "big one" that will rival the 8.2 magnitude quake that destroyed San Francisco in 1906.

When it does occur, according to a 1980 report by the Federal Emergency Management Agency, it is likely to kill between 3,000 and 12,500, put up to 50,000 in the hospital, leave 52,000 homeless over the long-term, and cause $25 billion in damage. Intense quakes along certain faults could be even more devastating.

Aside from damage caused directly from the quake, you may be threatened by fire from ruptured gas and electrical lines and water contamination due to broken mains. Utility service and food supplies are likely to be interrupted for some time and medical facilities will be over burdened. Not only should your home be structurally sound, but you should be prepared for the aftermath of a major quake, as covered below.

Location, Soil, Structure

When purchasing a home in areas prone to earthquakes you should consider its location in relation to faults, soil type, and structural soundness.

The U.S. Geological Survey and state geologists have extensively mapped earthquake faults and compiled historical records of their activity. Your real estate agent should be able to tell you whether a property is located on a fault and whether it is considered active. The Raymond Hill Fault in the San Gabriel Valley outside Los Angeles, for instance, is considered active and could cause the ground to rupture in a quake. It is covered with homes and apartment buildings, even though a recent California law requires that no structures be built within

50 feet of an active fault. The law addresses future development, but does not require people to evacuate homes and other buildings built in the past. Consequently, homes sit atop faults everywhere, even on the San Andreas fault.

When you look at a home, it probably will not be evident if it is on a fault, because the underlying rock formations where faults occur are generally covered with a deep layer of soil. When this top layer is loose alluvium, typical of river flood plains, or worse, landfill material, homes are more likely to be damaged in an earthquake. The reason: loose soil readily shifts. Many cities, including much of Los Angeles, have been built in river valleys characterized by alluvium, which also is prone to sliding away when the terrain is not flat. In addition, alluvium saturated with water can act like quicksand in a moderate to heavy earthquake, a phenomenon known as liquefaction. Structures actually can sink when this happens. While most people pay no heed to these factors when choosing a home, they will make a difference when the "big one" strikes.

Structural factors are also important. In earthquake country, never buy an unreinforced masonry home or one that stands on an unreinforced masonry foundation unless you are willing to bankroll major work that should be specified by an engineer. Also, check to see if the home is fastened to its foundation. Homes suffering from these structural defiencies are generally older and are the most likely to suffer major damage.

Strengthening Your Home to Minimize Damage

Masonry foundations, walls, chimneys and facades are likely to tumble in a moderate to heavy earthquake because they are rigid, heavy and consist of many small pieces. If you have masonry chimneys or facades on your home, back them with plywood and anchor them to the wood with metal ties, some of which should be nailed into the studs. Every one and one-half square feet of masonry surface should be anchored with ties spaced 12 inches apart. Anchoring an existing facade will involve disassembling the bricks and putting them back together. When doing so, make sure the mortar contains no more than 10 percent lime, otherwise it may be weak.

Figure 9-1

Securing Your Chimney

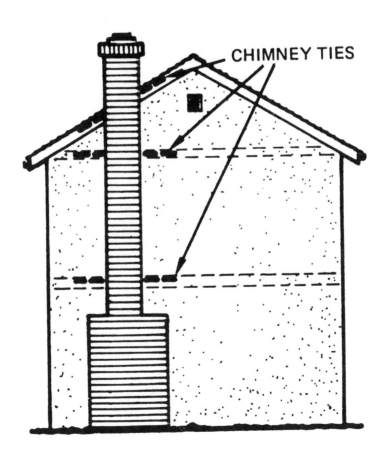

Exterior **chimneys should be strapped to the joists** of a home. Consult an engineer before having the work done. Unreinforced stone chimneys can be expected to tumble in a moderate to heavy quake. If the chimney potentially could fall through a roof and ceiling into the home, nail plywood on top of the ceiling joists around the chimney. Concrete block walls and foundations will hold up well as long as they are vertically and horizontally steel reinforced and fully grouted.

Woodframe homes are the most durable in earthquakes because they are flexible and light weight. Well-designed woodframe homes will have shear-walls of plywood or diagonal bracing. Also, they should be bolted to their foundations.

If a home is not bolted, do not despair because it is a simple and inexpensive job. You can even do it yourself with a masonry drill, a one-half-inch diameter carbide bit, a hammer, and seven-inch expansion anchor bolts that are one-half-inch in diameter. Drill through the wood sill, which sits atop the foundation every six feet in a one-story home and every four feet in a two-story home. Make sure there are holes within 12 inches of any joints in the sill. Tap the bolts in with a hammer after blowing the cement dust out of the drill holes with a plastic tube. Finally, tighten down the bolts with a wrench so they expand and bite into the foundation. Your home should now be well secured to its foundation.

Figure 9-2

Bolting Your House Down

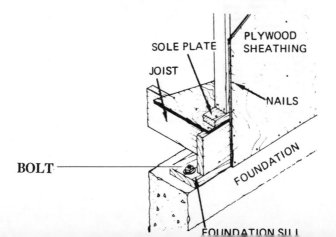

SOLE PLATE
PLYWOOD SHEATHING
JOIST
NAILS
FOUNDATION
BOLT
FOUNDATION SILL

Figure 9-3

Brace Yourself and Your Home

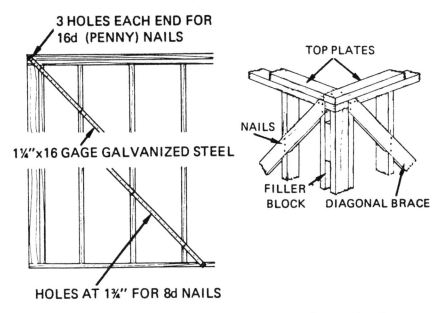

Other things that help prevent damage in an earthquake are:

● **Water heaters** strapped in with metal strips **anchored to wall studs;**

● **Flexible tubing** connecting appliances, such as stoves and dryers, to gas pipe outlets;

● **Spring-loaded latches** on kitchen cabinents; and

● L-shaped metal **braces connecting tall book cases** or cabinets to wall studs.

Other tips include making sure **heavy mirrors or pictures are fastened to studs** with closed eye hooks and keeping beds away from objects or furniture that could fall, including bookcases, pictures, and lamps. You may want to use thin plexiglass sheets instead of glass over framed prints and make sure hanging potted plants are lightweight. Lock your refrigerator's wheels in place or remove them altogether and tie it with braided wire at the top to hooks anchored in wall studs. Keep breakable household items low.

Preparing For The Aftermath

No matter how sound and secure your home is, you will be be faced with confusing and stressful situations in the aftermath of a major quake, such as power outages. Be prepared:

☐ Keep a **flashlight** in every bedroom;

☐ Know how to **cut off the electricity, gas and water** and keep an adjustable crescent wrench near the gas main and a pipe wrench near the water main;

☐ Keep extra **food and first aid** supplies;

☐ Keep **extra water** in airtight containers that are replaced every 12 months and keep water purification tablets on hand;

☐ Be prepared to cook on a **camping stove** or barbecue (have one and have adequate fuel and matches);

☐ Keep a **portable radio** with fresh batteries to hear important news broadcasts;

☐ Keep a **fire extinguisher;**

☐ **Learn first aid;** and

☐ Have a **game plan** for uniting family members who may be caught at work or school.

Utmost, follow the instructions of public safety officials. By exercising these precautions and assuring that your home is structurally sound, chances are excellent that you will survive a major earthquake without injury.

CHECKLIST FOR EARTHQUAKES

Structural Soundness:

☐ Masonry construction or foundations are unsound.

☐ Masonry chimneys and facades should be fastened to home's frame and prevented from falling through the ceiling.

☐ Wood frame walls should be diagonally braced.

☐ Wood frame homes should be bolted to their foundations.

☐ Water heaters, tall furniture and refrigerators should be secured to wall studs.

☐ Cement block construction should be steel reinforced.

☐ Pictures, mirrors, and other household items should be properly secured.

For The Aftermath:

☐ Have extra food, water and first aid supplies.

☐ Have flashlights, portable radio, and fresh batteries.

☐ Have game plan for reuniting family members.

☐ Know how to cut off gas, electricity and water.

☐ Have a fire extinguisher.

☐ Be prepared to give first aid.

Chapter Ten

Noise

One quiet April morning in 1964 a cacaphony of jack-hammers jarred residents of New York City's Sixth Avenue from restful sleep. For the next three years, their lives would never be the same because the Slattery Construction Co., eventually dubbed "Slattery's Army," had broken ground on a subway extension project.

Remembering the day in his 1970 book *The Tyranny of Noise*, Robert Alex Baron wrote, "Suddenly all hell broke loose. What someone later termed 'a symphony of insanity' had begun. The overture to a three year concert combined the sounds of air compressors, jackhammers, rock drills, chain saws and dynamite blasts, with additional instrumentation by cement mixers, vibrators, cranes and portable generators."

But as Baron showed in his popular manifesto, noise pollution was not confined to the New York City borough of Manhattan. Indeed it was a national issue, affecting millions of Americans right in their homes. Disquieted by the din of freeways, airports, construction work, power mowers and equipment, Congress in 1970 passed the Noise Pollution and Abatement Act, directing EPA to study the problem of noise pollution. When the agency reported its findings, Congress passed the Noise Control Act of 1972, calling on EPA to determine acceptable levels of urban noise and set design standards to reduce noise from new equipment.

Throughout the remainder of the decade, noise studies, standards, abatement strategies, and ordinances poured forth. Yet in 1980, EPA warned that 93 million people lived in urban areas where noise levels still exceeded the acceptable daily average of 55 decibels. And this did not include those living near airports and freeways.

In the same report, EPA concluded that community noise levels would rise as U.S. cities and suburbs become more densely populated, a trend particularly problemmatical if you are one of the millions of workers exposed to deafening noise levels on the job. You can expect that it will be increasingly difficult to rest your ears, even at home. Moreover, accumulating data indicate that high noise levels are associated with stress, heart disease, sleep disruption, and lack of mental concentration. Despite this evidence, the federal government closed down EPA's noise office in a $14 million a year cost-cutting move just one year after the 1980 report was issued.

As an individual, you are left largely to protect yourself and family from noise and the only place you have control is at home. If you are buying a home, you should consider noise levels in any prospective neighborhood. If you already own a home in a noisy neighborhood, you may want to consider some soundproofing measures.

Understanding Noise

One person's noise is another person's music, as the saying goes. A hot saxaphone solo blaring from a stereo at midnight is melodic to the jazz aficionado, but disturbing if you dislike jazz and are trying to go to sleep. And so it is that acoustic experts define noise as unwanted sound that distracts, disturbs or interrupts everyday activities, such as sleep, conversation, reading or listening to the television or radio.

Sound itself occurs when mechanical vibration creates waves of vibration in the air. As these waves travel, they lose energy, so a sound is always loudest at its source. The ear translates the air waves into nervous energy, which is perceived and interpreted by the brain.

While people generally consider sound either soft or loud, scientists measure it on a logarithmic scale in units of intensity called decibels. Any sound above zero decibels is audible when your hearing is normal. However, there is not a one-to-one correspondence in loudness and intensity, or decibel level. Indeed, loudness doubles with each increase of ten decibels, so a sound that is 60 decibels is twice as loud as a sound that is 50 decibels and four times as loud as a sound that is 40 decibels.

Normal speech generally has an intesity of around 70 decibels when measured at a distance of one foot. A loud motorcycle at 50 feet will have an intensity of almost 100 decibels, about eight times as loud. A jet take-off produces a sound approaching 130 decibels at 200 feet, which is above the 120 decibel threshold of pain.

Several sources of sound in an area produce ambient, or background noise. In a study, EPA found that noise levels average 50 decibels in quiet suburban neighborhoods, 55 decibels in normal suburban neighborhoods, 60 decibels in urban residential areas, 65 decibels in noisy urban neighborhoods, and 70 decibels in very noisy urban neighborhoods. Aircraft and major highways add to noise levels in any of these settings.

Health Effects of Noise

Hearing loss from exposure to noise is one of the most prevalent occupational diseases in the United States, with more than 15 million Americans exposed to deafening levels of noise on the job. Consistent exposure to levels above 75 decibels averaged over eight hours, typical of many workplace environments, can cause hearing loss, according to EPA. Even if you have a quiet job, you have a good chance of being exposed to an average level of 75 decibels, because of transportation noise and noise at home.

Prolonged exposure to excessive levels of noise damages the hair cells in the inner ear, which translate sound into the nerve signals that are interpreted by the brain. Brief exposure to loud noises can cause temporary loss of hearing. But even though there are thousands of hair cells, their ability to heal is limited. With repeated exposure, eventually they die and the ability to hear is diminished.

However, the effects of noise are not limited to hearing loss. Noise breeds an involuntary response akin to fear. Your heart beats faster and adrenalin is released to prepare you to fight or take flight. While you have learned through experience not to fight or run, changes in your heart rate and adrenalin levels occur involuntarily. The result is that noise increases your level of stress, which is known to cause heart disease.

A number of studies have linked exposure to excessive noise and high blood pressure and heart disease. For instance, an eight-year study completed in 1983 showed that heart attack rates were 18 percent higher for people 75 years of age or older living near Los Angeles International Airport. Outdoor noise levels in the neighborhoods studied averaged 90 decibels, the level at which industrial workers must wear hearing protection devices.

A study conducted by EPA and the National Institutes of Health under controlled laboratory conditions clearly showed that rhesus monkeys develop high blood pressure when exposed to the levels of noise many Americans experience daily. These and other studies led EPA to conclude that noise may be a contributor to heart disease and stroke, which together kill almost half of all Americans.

Finally, studies have shown that noise disrupts sleep and makes it more difficult to concentrate in school and on the job. In general, the evidence indicates that noise adds to both the physiological and psychological stress that is characteristic of modern urban life. Yet, many people do not perceive noise as a source of stress.

Scoping A Neighborhood For Noise

At home, the sources of noise are many, from appliances and power gardening equipment to nearby industries, traffic and airports. If you are highly sensitive to noise, you can choose to forgo modern appliances and substitute your own labor in household chores. You also can insulate and dampen the noise from appliances. However, the remainder of this chapter will focus primarily on how to fight noises generated outside your home.

First, if you are looking for a home to buy, make sure

to survey the neighborhood for sources of noise. Is there a freeway or busy boulevard nearby? A railyard or train tracks? An airport or military base? A factory? A warehouse or store where goods will be shipped and received while truck engines are idling? An electrical utility transformer station? These are some of the common sources of disruptive noise.

Second, remember that noise generated by these facilities will not be constant, but will vary with their operation. For instance, goods may be delivered at night to a supermarket that backs a house you are considering, potentially disrupting your sleep. Or a factory may not be operating on the weekend when you are looking at a home.

Third, if there is a source of noise, check with your local government to see if it is regulated in a way that is acceptable to you. Many cities and counties have adopted noise regulations that attempt to prevent disruptive noise through measures such as banning delivery of goods at night or limiting airport operations. Also, if a house is near a freeway, check with your state or county highway department to see if a noise barrier is planned. Barriers along freeways have substantially cut noise in nearby homes. In fact, if you are willing to endure freeway noise until a barrier is constructed you may actually get a better buy on a home, since noise tends to depress property values.

Fourth, check on background noise by opening the windows when you look at a house. Remember, a closed up house will be much quieter than one with the windows open. Will the noise level be disruptive? Also, sit outside on the patio or porch and listen. Will the noise bother you and make it unattractive to sit outside? Remember too that noise from a highway will vary with traffic flow. Weekday rush hours will be considerably louder than Sunday morning.

Following these steps will help you to understand and evaluate the noise levels in a prospective neighborhood. While you may discount the noise factor in the end, at least you will not be surprised by it as are thousands each year who regret they did not consider noise levels before buying homes.

Soundproofing

If you own a home and outdoor noise is a problem, you can take some steps to restore peace of mind.

Storm windows or double windows will cut down on noise entering your home, as will a tight air seal on your windows. When an ordinary window is closed, it will eliminate between 15 and 20 decibels of noise entering through that area. A double window will eliminate 20 decibels when opened in staggered fashion and 30 to 35 decibels when shut. When both shut and fitted to be airtight, a double window will cut noise by 35 to 45 decibels.

Another technique is to insulate the walls and attic of your home. Often, you can achieve a substantial reduction in road noise, for instance, by insulating just those walls facing the roadway. Attic insulation helps reduce jet noise.

Weatherproofing exterior doors and filling any air leaks in walls will help cut noise too. And at once noise enters, you can minimize its reverberation by having carpets, drapes and stuffed furniture in your home.

Outdoors, you can build your own sound wall between a patio, for instance, and a roadway. Construct the wall out of cement blocks and disguise it by piling up dirt to form a berm that can be planted as a garden.

All of these steps will help cut noise, but they can be fairly expensive. Soundproofing, including steps to reduce inside noise such as damping on appliances, can cost between two and 10 percent of the value of a home. The lesson? It is better to avoid purchasing a home near a noisy highway or airport to begin with.

CHECKLIST FOR NOISE

Scoping the Neighborhood:

    ☐ Look for facilities that cause noise:

        ☐ Airports;

        ☐ Highways;

        ☐ Rail facilities;

        ☐ Electrical transformers;

        ☐ Factories; and

        ☐ Warehouses or loading docks.

    ☐ Check on their regulation with local government

    ☐ Is background noise tolerable?

        ☐ Open the windows and listen.

        ☐ Sit outside and listen.

Soundproofing Measures:

    ☐ Double windows that are airtight;

    ☐ Weatherproofing on doors;

    ☐ Filling cracks and gaps;

    ☐ Wall and ceiling insulation; and

    ☐ Sound walls around outdoor sitting areas.

Chapter Eleven

Selecting Laboratories

and Contractors

After personally screening your property or prospective home for environmental problems and contacting public agencies to obtain information, it is time to decide which, if any, contaminants to test for. In retaining a testing laboratory, and if you have any problems a contractor, you need to be cognizant of several factors. Before incurring the expense of environmental testing be sure to take these steps:

• Discuss any potential problem with your state or local environmental or public health agency to get their advice. They may have valuable information on your neighborhood, such as studies of lead in soil or drinking water or presence of asbestos in homes. Ask for the public affairs or community relations department, which will expedite your inquiry.

• For wellwater, contact your state or local health department and water resources agency to see if either has tested wells in your area. Rather than reinventing the wheel by testing yourself, you may obtain both quickly and free of charge a good profile of contamination in your well. You can also obtain advice about treatment techniques.

• For potential indoor air pollution problems from gas burning appliances, call your gas company. It will likely inspect the appliances and measure pollutants, such as carbon monoxide, free of charge.

After taking these steps, you are ready to select a laboratory.

Selecting a Testing Laboratory

A testing laboratory will provide you with a single numerical value for any contaminant. If it exceeds the existing health standard, the test indicates you have a problem. If it is below the standard, you are free and clear. Sounds good, but think again.

Analytical chemistry is akin to cooking and as any cook knows there are good meals and bad meals. A chemist, like a cook, can make any number of blunders between taking a sample and providing test results. The sample must be taken in an appropriate container that will not react with the contaminants. It must then be handled properly—perhaps refrigerated and kept out of light—to prevent some contaminants from breaking down. It must be analyzed in a timely manner with equipment that is properly calibrated. It must be properly tracked to prevent samples from being mixed up. And there are many more considerations too technical to discuss here.

Increased concern about environmental contamination has prompted a boom in the laboratory services field. The American Council of Independent Laboratories reported its members enjoyed up to a 40 percent increase in the environmental testing business in 1988 alone. "In the environmental testing area, our members have been scrambling to keep up with demand," said a council official. "The environmental market is expected to continue strong for a number of years, possibly for the next decade."

But while the boom has been good for the laboratory industry's bottom line, the quick growth has created problems too, such as backlogs, finding qualified personnel, and controlling quality. A 1989 study by the consumer group Public Citizen, for instance, found that three of the largest radon testing laboratories in the U.S. erred on 25 percent of the test kits they analyzed. Since both your health and money are riding on the accuracy of test results, exercise caution in selecting a laboratory.

Here are some useful tips.

• Call the federal Environmental Protection Agency or your state environmental agency (Appendix) for a list of testing firms in your area. For some types of tests, EPA and state agencies have certified laboratories. You also should ask these agencies which laboratories they use in your area, if any, and which test methods or protocols should be observed for individual contaminants.

• If selecting laboratories from the Yellow Pages, make sure to ask for their certifications and what test methods or protocols they intend to use. If a laboratory representative balks or is unfamiliar with an EPA or state protocol, find another firm.

• At once you have a list of qualified firms, call for price information, turn around times, and information on how they will collect and analyze samples. Ask for a description of quality control procedures. Some calibration standard should be used.

• Make sure you specify that your final report provide more than a list of contaminants and their concentrations. Ask for quality control data and raw data, such as a chromatogram or spectrometry diagram. Make sure the report indicates it is your sample by providing chain-of-custody information. If the report indicates no detectable level of a contaminant, make sure it specifies the laboratory's detection limit. Retain the report for your records should any dispute or problem arise at a later date. Also, just as auto maintenance records are handy when you sell your car, the test report will be valuable if you sell your house.

Choosing a Contractor

You need to exercise equal caution in choosing a contractor to solve an environmental problem. On the whole, contractors are honest and capable, but as a consumer you need to be wary of incompetent and fly-by-night operators. In a recent sting, the Florida Department of Professional Regulation netted 160 unlicensed contractors operating in the Tampa Bay area alone. And concerns over competence led the Florida Deparment of Health to set standards for radon mitigation contractors and personel.

Here are some tips for selecting a contractor.

• First, call EPA and your state environmental or public health agency for a list of contractors that specialize in solving your particular problem. Many states require certification for environmental services, such as asbestos removal, septic tank maintenance and radon work.

• After identifying candidates in your area, contact them, explain what you need, and ask for: 1) a statement of qualifications, listing previous jobs performed with references; 2) professional and financial references; 3) information on insurance coverage and bonding and 4) evidence of licenses and certfications.

• Then, call and make sure the contractor is financially solvent, has a good reputation among the professional community, and has performed well on previous jobs.

• The contractor should have general liability insurance. Check for any exclusions. In the case of asbestos removal, the policy should be "occurrence-type" rather than "claims-made," since asbestos-related diseases generally develop slowly. Occurrence-type coverage provides long-term protection, where claims-made insurance is valid for a limited period. In addition, the contractor should have asbestos insurance.

● Check the contractor's record with licensing authorities for violations. Also check with the local Better Business Bureau.

● Interview the contractor and the person who will be managing the job.

● Get competitive bids, but remember that cost is not the only consideration. Bids that are considerably lower than others may mean a contractor plans to cut corners. It is best if a bid quotes a maximum guaranteed cost.

● Final bids should include a detailed work plan and if asbestos is being removed, remember there should be a final air monitoring report by an independent laboratory. The final bid should also specify the materials that will be used; a project completion date; proof of liability insurance and workmen's compensation; an explanation of permits, inspections, and fees required; and payment terms.

● Finally, expect that before providing detailed bids, a contractor will ask you to provide information on your ability to pay for the job. You should respect this as a good business practice.

Before signing a contract, read it carefully for loopholes, omissions and ambiguities. Make sure specifications are clear, including, for instance, the model and size of an air exchanger needed to solve an indoor air pollution problem. You should also make sure that:

● The contract references any architectural or engineering drawings and that both you and the contractor have these;

● Proof of insurance is attached; and

● Final payment is not made until after the job is finished and that the amount of this payment is substantial enough to ensure that the contractor finishes the final details.

You also want to make sure that the contractor's suppliers do not come after you if they are not paid. You can accomplish this by attaching a "waiver of mechanic's lien" to the contract or by making the final payment contingent upon receiving the contractor's receipts for all materials, equipment, and labor used for the job.

The contract should include a clause guaranteeing the work against defects. In the case of reducing levels of radon or again asbestos, you should make sure this clause provides that levels will meet applicable numerically enumerated standards after the work is finished. Make sure both you and the contractor initial any contract changes. Finally, make sure to obtain any product or material warranties from your contractor.

If you are not satisfied with the job, you can place the final payment into an escrow account through an attorney, title company, or some banks until the contractor rectifies the deficiencies. In the case of cost overruns, remember that the contractor cannot compel you to pay more than specified in the contract.

When a contract dispute cannot be resolved, you can start by filing a complaint with the Better Business Bureau. The next steps are to seek arbitration, or to file suit in either small claims court or other court, depending on the amount of money involved.

By observing these steps and considerations, you will help protect yourself against incompetence and potential fraud when retaining the services of laboratories and contractors.

CHECKLIST FOR SELECTING LABORATORIES

AND CONTRACTORS

<u>Laboratories:</u>

☐ Check with EPA and state agencies for suggestions.

☐ Check on certifications and test methods.

☐ Specify a full test report.

<u>Contractors:</u>

☐ Obtain qualifications, references, and evidence of licenses, certifications and insurance.

☐ Check record of violations and complaints.

☐ Check references and financial position.

☐ Make sure insurance is adequate.

☐ Interview contractor.

☐ Get competitive bids.

☐ Make sure contract is complete and without loopholes or ambiguities.

☐ Make final payment contingent upon satisfactory completion of job.

Chapter Twelve

How to Buy an

Environmentally

Safe Home

Negotiating cleanup of toxic hazards has become standard practice in commercial real estate transactions as knowledge of the environmental health risks lurking in buildings has grown in the 1980s. Billions of dollars are being spent to remove asbestos, control radon and solve other environmental problems in the wake of laws and court decisions that clearly establish building owners are responsible for eliminating toxic hazards.

Concern over environmental hazards has changed the nature of real estate transactions, but so far the changes have been restricted primarily to commercial and industrial properties. Purchasers routinely inspect these properties for environmental problems and use inspection data in negotiating price and terms. Sophisticated business buyers know that in any transaction information is power, in this case the power to protect the health of workers and customers and avoid unforeseen liabilities. But how about when you buy a home? Shouldn't you enjoy equal protection?

The fact is you do not. There are almost no laws that explicitly protect you despite that studies, discussed in previous chapters, have repeatedly found exposure to toxics in the home is actually greater than anywhere else for many people. Only you can protect yourself by seeking to uncover toxic hazards when shopping for a home and using that information.

Finding out if a home has a toxic problem and obtaining a rough estimate for solving it will allow you to answer these important questions:

- Do I want to buy the home at all?

- Can I afford to solve the problem after purchasing it?

- Will the seller negotiate on the price or terms of sale before entering a purchase agreement?

Warning: You will not find it easy to negotiate a solution to a toxic problem in the overheated real estate market of a quickly growing metropolis, such as Washington, Los Angeles or Toronto. The seller generally will want you to take the property as is. But try it anyway, since you have nothing to lose. In stable markets you are likely to have some luck, particularly with such well-known contaminants as radon and asbestos.

So take a lesson from commercial real estate moguls and try these strategies when buying a home. Remember, you stand completely alone in protecting your family's health.

First, examine the home yourself for potential problems using the checklists and information in previous chapters. Frankly discuss environmental concerns, such as pesticide usage, with the real estate agent and seller. Ask the agent about state laws, if any, that require disclosure or testing. Also ask for any environmental test results, such as radon levels. If you want to buy the home, decide which contaminants are most likely to present problems and incorporate appropriate contingency language into your purchase offer, just as you would for structural inspection and defects. Discuss what you want with your attorney.

EPA recommends that all homes be tested for radon. Moreover, it should be standard practice to test wellwater for bacteria, have septic tanks checked and in California and other active fault zones have the structural inspector check for earthquake soundness. Remember, environmental tests will take time. If a problem turns up, such as friable asbestos or wellwater contamination, get cost estimates for needed work. Your basic options are to:

- Require the seller to resolve the problem before closing a deal;

- Seek a price reduction equivalent to the cost of needed work;

- Walk away from the deal if the seller will not negotiate; or

- Close the deal and finance the work yourself.

One factor to remember is that once an environmental problem is discovered the real estate agent may have a legal duty to disclose it to other interested buyers. In fact, real estate agents are usually bound by one of three standards, depending upon the state, when it comes to disclosing material defects in a home. Under the strict liability standard, you may be able to successfully sue the agent if you find, for instance, elevated levels of radon in your home that are not disclosed before the sale. Under the diligent inspection and disclosure standard, the agent must have a reasonably competent inspection performed and disclose any defects uncovered. Under the simple negligence standard, an inspection is not always required. Often, it is sufficient simply to inquire when there is reasonable doubt concerning a seller's representation.

Do not get too excited, though, because there is no government agency out enforcing these standards. If you run into a problem your only remedy is through individual legal action, which takes time and money. Moreover, it remains unclear how these standards apply in residential real estate transactions where environmental contamination is found.

Concern is growing in the real estate industry. The National Association of Realtors has cautioned its members to discuss radon when listing a property. "The purchase of a home is an extraordinarily significant, expensive and personal experience," advises Ralph Holmen, an attorney with the association's office of the chief counsel. "Injection of what most people regard as an unusual and unfamiliar consideration—the actual or potential presence of a possibly carcinogenic substance in the home —is frightening." Yet, he continues, "real estate professionals, and the sellers they represent, should consider radon testing prior to the time a buyer requests such results or testing otherwise appears necessary. Advance testing makes disclosure to the buyer more convenient and credible and often expedites the processes of negotiation and purchase."

But radon is just one of many possible contaminants. Unfortunately, there has been little talk within the real estate industry of others, such as lead in soil. Again, you are your best protector.

If you cannot test before closing a deal, try negotiating an escrow account in which some of the money from the transaction will remain until specified environmental tests are performed. If these tests show there is a contamination problem after you take occupancy, the money can be used to pay for needed work.

You should specify that septic tanks, heat exchangers, dehumidifiers, and air conditioning and heating systems will work without problem for at least 30 days and are installed in conformance with any codes. If these break down, the seller should make necessary repairs or replacements.

Policy Changes Needed

It is difficult to conclude without advocating modest public policy steps to provide better protection against toxic exposure in the home. While the individual can safeguard himself, it is ironic that federal laws, such as the Superfund, require billions of dollars to clean up toxic waste dumps that often present only a negligible health hazard, while contaminants in the home are almost completely unaddressed. It is even more ironic that homes being built today will present toxic health hazards long into the future because readily available non-toxic construction materials and designs—such as pine sheathing and masonry plywood absent of forldehyde, non-toxic interior finishes and foundation vacuum systems to eliminate radon—are not being employed.

To improve protection:

● The federal Environmental Protection Agency and state authorities should step up their efforts to inform the public, home builders, realtors, and local officials of toxic contamination in and around the home;

● EPA and state environmental authorities should step up research on the extent of toxic contamination in homes and do more to develop and promote both techniques for solving existing problems and model construction codes that will minimize toxics when new homes are built;

● EPA and the Consumer Product Safety Commission should step up efforts to set standards for construction materials and home furnishings that minimize toxic constituents;

● EPA should develop more information about the use of pesticides in homes and neighborhoods and take action to restrict products that pose unreasonable risks; and

● States should require disclosure of lead levels in tap water, the presence and state of asbestos and radon levels when homes are sold, as well as earthquake soundness in active fault areas.

These steps would build on existing programs and efforts, stopping short of massive expenditures and a new layer of intrusive regulation. Primarily they would provide useful information enabling the private sector and, most important, the individual to solve the problem of toxic contamination in the home.

APPENDIX: Canada

In Canada, information is available from both Environment Canada and provincial agencies. Contact Environment Canada for information and tips on which provincial agency may also be able to help.

Communications Office
Atlantic Region
Environment Canada
45 Alderney Drive
Dartmouth, Nova Scotia B2Y 2N6

Communications Office
Quebec Region
Environment Canada
3 Buade Street
PO Box 606
Quebec, Quebec G1R 4V7

Communications Office
Ontario Region
Environment Canada
25 St. Clair Avenue East
6th Floor
Toronto, Ontario M4T 1M2

Communications Office
Western and Northern Region
Environment Canada
2nd Floor
Twin Atria 2
4999-98 Avenue
Edmonton, Alberta T6B 2X3

Communications Office
Pacific and Yukon Region
Environment Canada
3rd Floor
Kapilano 100—Park Royal South
West Vancouver, B.C. V7T 1A2

APPENDIX: For Further Information

This appendix provides a list of government agencies that may be of help in providing specific information in your area, including helpful tips ranging from lists of certified contractors to what types of contaminants are found in wells.

Remember that government agencies are big and you may be transferred several times on the telephone before you reach the right person. However, government staff generally are helpful, so be patient.

Unless you can find the appropriate state agency, start with a federal hotline or the nearest Environmental Protection Agency regional office. They should be able to provide you with useful information, including state contacts.

Federal Agencies

Consumer Product Safety Commission (Provides information on asbestos products and other products in the home.)
(800) 638-2772
(800) 492-8363 in Maryland
(800) 638-8333 in Alaska, Hawaii, Puerto Rico, Virgin Islands

Environmental Protection Agency:

Asbestos Hotline:
(Provides information on asbestos analysis laboratories) (800) 334-8571 ext. 6741

Chemical Emergency Preparedness Program Hotline: (Provides information on how to find out about your community preparedness plan for releases of toxic chemicals.)
(800) 535-0202
(202) 479-2449 Washington, D.C. and Alaska

National Pesticides Telecommunications Network: (Provides information 24 hours a day on pesticide problems.)
(800) 858-7378
(806) 743-3091 in Texas

Resource Conservation and Recovery Act/Superfund Hotline: (Provides information on hazardous waste disposal facilities and) abandoned hazardous waste sites.) (8 (202) 382-3000 in Washington, D.C.

EPA Regional Offices (Provide general information and tips on which agencies to contact in your state for your particular problem):

EPA Region 1
Room 2203
JFK Federal Building
Boston, MA 02203
(617) 223-4845
(Connecticut, Maine, Massachusetts, New Hampshire, Rhode Island,

Vermont)

EPA Region 2
26 Federal Plaza
New York, NY 10278
(212) 264-2515
(New Jersey, New York, Puerto
Rico, Virgin Islands)

EPA Region 3
841 Chestnut Street
Philadelphia, PA 19107
(215) 597-8320
(Delaware, District of Columbia,
Maryland, Pennsylvania, Virginia,
West Virginia)

EPA Region 4
345 Courtland Street, NE
Atlanta, GA 30365
(404) 881-3776
(Alabama, Florida, Georgia,
Kentucky, Mississippi, North
Carolina, South Carolina,
Tennessee)

EPA Region 5
230 South Dearborn Street
Chicago, IL 60604
(312) 353-2205
(Illinois, Indiana, Michigan,
Minnesota, Ohio, Wisconsin)

EPA Region 6
1201 Elm Street
Dallas, TX 75270
(214) 767-2630
(Arkansas, Louisiana, New Mexico,
Oklahoma, Texas)

EPA Region 7
726 Minnesota Avenue
Kansas City, KS 66101
(913) 236-2803
(Iowa, Kansas, Missouri, Nebraska)

EPA Region 8
Suite 1300
One Denver Place
999 18th Street
Denver, CO 80202
(303) 283-1710
(Colorado, Montana, North Dakota,
South Dakota, Utah, Wyoming)

EPA Region 9
215 Fremont Street
San Francisco, CA 94105
(415) 974-8076
(Arizona, California, Hawaii,
Nevada)

EPA Region 10
1200 Sixth Avenue
Seattle, WA 98101
(206) 442-7660
(Alaska, Idaho, Oregon,
Washington)

State Agencies

Alabama:

Radon

Radiological Health Branch
Alabama Department of Public Health
State Office Building
Montgomery, AL 36130
(205) 261-5315

Water

Water Supply Branch
Department of Environmental Management
1751 Federal Drive
Montgomery, AL 36130
(205) 271-7773

Alaska:

Radon

Radiological Health Program
Alaska Department of Health and Social Services
Box H-06F
Juneau, AK 99811-0613
(907) 465-3019

Water

Alaska Drinking Water Program
Water Quality Management
Department of Environmental Conservation
PO Box O
Juneau, AK 99811
(907) 465-2653

Arizona:

Asbestos

Department of Environmental Quality
Office of Air Quality
2005 North Central Avenue
Phoenix, AZ 85004
(602) 257-2285

Radon

Arizona Radiation Regulatory Agency
4814 South 40th Street
Phoenix, AZ 85040
(602) 255-4845

Water

Compliance Unit
Waste and Water Quality Management
Room 202
2005 North Central Avenue
Phoenix, AZ 85004

(602) 257-2235

Arkansas:

Radon

Division of Radiation Control
Arkansas Department of Public Health
4815 West Markham Street
Little Rock, AR 72205-3867
(501) 661-2301

Water

Division of Engineering
Arkansas State Health Department
4815 West Markham Street
Little Rock, AR 72201-3867
(501) 661-2000

California:

Radon

California Department of Health Services
Room 334
2151 Berkeley Way
Berkeley, CA 94704
(415) 540-2469

Radiation Management
County of Los Angeles
Department of Health Services
2615 South Grand Avenue
Los Angeles, CA 90007
(213) 744-3244

Water

Sanitary Engineering Branch
Department of Health Services
Room 600
714 P Street
Sacramento, CA 95814
(916) 323-6111

Colorado:

Asbestos

Colorado Department of Health
4210 East 11th Street
Denver, CO 80220
(303) 331-8587

Radon

Radiation Control Division
Colorado Department of Health
4210 East 11th Avenue
Denver, CO 80220

(303) 331-4812

Water

Drinking Water Section
Colorado Department of Health
4210 East 11th Avenue
Denver, CO 80220
(303) 320-8333

Connecticut:

Radon

Radon Program
Toxic Hazards Section
Connecticut Department of Health Services
150 Washington Street
(203) 566-3122

Water

Water Supply Section
Connecticut Department of Health
79 Elm Street
Hartford, CT 06115
(203) 566-1251

Delaware:

Radon

Division of Public Health
Delaware Bureau of Environmental Health
PO Box 637
Dover, DE 19901
(302) 736-4731

Water

Office of Sanitary Engineering
Division of Public Health
Jesse Cooper Memorial Building
Capital Square
Dover, DE 19901
(302) 736-4731

District of Columbia:

Radon   Department of Consumer and Regulatory Affairs
614 H Street, NW
Room 1014
Washington, DC 2001
(202) 727-7728

Water

Water Hygiene Branch
Department of Consumer and Regulatory Affairs
5010 Overlook Avenue, SW
Washington, DC 20032

(202) 767-7370

Florida:

Radon   Environmental Radiation Control Laboratory
        Department of Health and Rehabilitative Services
                             1317 Winewood Blvd.
                       Tallahassee, FL 32399-0700
                                 (904) 487-1004

Water   Department of Environmental Regulation
                           Twin Towers Office Building
                                2600 Blair Stone Road
                           Tallahassee, FL 32301-8241
                                 (904) 487-1779

Georgia:

Radon   Environmental Protection Division
              Georgia Department of Human Resources
                             878 Peachtree Street
                                     Room 100
                              Atlanta, GA 30309
                                 (404) 894-6644

Water   Water Protection Branch
                      Environmental Protection Division
                       Department of Natural Resources
                         270 Washington Street, SW
                              Atlanta, GA 30334
                                 (404) 656-3530

Hawaii:

Asbestos   Environmental Protection
                             State Health Department
                                     PO Box 3378
                                Honolulu, HI 96801
                                 (808) 548-6455

Radon   Environmental Protection
                         Hawaii Department of Health
                             591 Ala Moana Blvd.
                                Honolulu, HI 96813
                                 (808) 549-4383

Water   Drinking Water Program
                                     Sanitation Branch
                              Environmental Protection

PO Box 3378
Honolulu, HI 96801
(808) 548-4682

Idaho:

Radon

Bureau of Preventative Medicine
Division of Health
Idaho Department of Health and Welfare
450 West State Street
Boise, ID 83720
(208) 334-5927

Water

Water Quality Bureau
Division of Environment
Idaho Department of Health and Welfare
Statehouse
Boise, ID 83720
(208) 334-5867

Illinois:

Asbestos

Asbestos Abatement Program
Illinois Department of Public Health
525 W. Jefferson St.
Third Floor
Springfield, IL 62761
(217) 782-3517

Radon

Illinois Department of Nuclear Safety
Office of Environmental Safety
1301 Knotts Street
Springfield, IL 62703
(217) 786-6384

Water

Division of Public Water Supplies
Illinois Environmental Protection Agency
2200 Churchill Road
Springfield, IL 62706
(217) 785-8653

Indiana:

Asbestos

Office of Air Management
Department of Environmental Management
105 South Meridian Street
PO Box 6015
Indianapolis, IN 46206-6015
(317) 232-8232

Radon

Division of Industrial Hygiene and Health
Indiana State Board of Health
1330 W. Michigan Street
PO Box 1964
Indianapolis, IN 46206-1964
(317) 633-0153

Water

Division of Public Water Supply
Indiana State Board of Health
1330 West Michigan Street
Indianapolis, IN 46206-1964
(317) 633-0174

Iowa:

Radon

Bureau of Radiological Health
Iowa Department of Public Health
Lucas State Office Building
Des Moines, IA 50319-0075
(515) 281-7781

Water

Water Supply Section
Surface and Groundwater Protection Bureau
Iowa Department of Natural Resources
Henry A. Wallace Building
900 East Grand
Des Moines, IA 50319
(515) 281-8998

Kansas:

Asbestos

Department of Health and Environment
Forbes Field
Topeka, KS 66620
(913) 296-1544

Radon

Radiation Control Program
Bureau of Air Quality and Radiation Control
Kansas Department of Health and Environment
Forbes Field
Building 740
Topeka, KS 66620-0110
(913) 296-1560

Water

Bureau of Water Protection
Kansas Department of Health and Environment
Forbes Field
Building 740
Topeka, KS 66620
(913) 862-9360

Kentucky:

Radon

Radiation Control Branch
Division of Radiation and Product Safety
Department of Health Services
Cabinet for Human Resources
275 East Main Street
Frankfort, KY 40621
(502) 564-3700

Water

Division of Water
Department of Environmental Protection
18 Reilly Road
Fort Boone Plaza
Frankfort, KY 40601
(502) 564-3410

Louisiana:

Radon

Louisiana Nuclear Energy Division
PO Box 14690
Baton Rouge, LA 70898-4690
(504) 925-4518

Water   Office of Preventive and Public Health Services
Louisiana Department of Health and Human Resources
PO Box 60630
New Orleans, LA 70160
(504) 568-5105

Maine:

Radon

Indoor Air Program
Division of Health Engineering
Maine Department of Human Services
State House Station 10
Augusta, ME 04333
(207) 289-3826

Water

Department of Human Services
Bureau of Health
Division of Health Engineering
State House
Augusta, ME 04333
(207) 289-3826

Maryland:

Asbestos
Maryland Department of the Environment
201 West Preston Street
Room 214
Baltimore, MD 21201
(301) 225-5753

Radon
Center for Radiological Health
Maryland Department of Environment
2500 Broening Highway
Baltimore, MD 21224
(301) 631-3300

Water
Division of Water Supplies
Inspection and Compliance Program
Department of Health and Mental Hygiene
Office of Environmental Programs
201 West Preston Street
Baltimore, MD 21201
(301) 225-6360

Massachusetts:

Radon
Radiation Control Program
Massachusetts Department of Public Health
23 Service Center
North Hampton, MA 01060
(413) 586-7525
(617) 727-6214 in Boston

Water
Division of Water Supply
Department of Environmental Quality Engineering
One Winter Street
Boston, MA 02108
(617) 292-5770

Michigan:

Asbestos
Department of Public Health
Division of Occupational Health
Attention: Asbestos Program
3500 N. Logan Street
PO Box 30035
Lansing, MI 48909
(517) 335-8250

Radon
Division of Radiological Health
Michigan Department of Public Health
3423 North Logan
PO Box 30195

Lansing, MI 48909
(517) 335-8190

Water   Water Supply Services Division
Environmental and Occupational Health Services
Administration
3500 North Logan Street
PO Box 30035
Lansing, MI 48909
(517) 335-8318

Minnesota:

Radon   Section of Radiation Control
Environmental Health Division
Minnesota Department of Health
717 Delaware Street, SE
PO Box 9441
Minneapolis, MN 55440
(612) 623-5348

Water   Section of Public Water Supplies
Minnesota Department of Health
717 Delaware Street
Minneapolis, MN 55440
(612) 623-5330

Mississippi:

Radon   Division of Radiological Health
Mississippi Department of Health
3150 Lawson Street
PO Box 1700
Jackson, MS 39215-1700
(601) 354-6657

Water   Division of Water Supply
State Board of Health
PO Box 1700
Jackson, MS 39205
(601) 354-6616 or 490-4211

Missouri:

Asbestos   Bureau of Environmental Epidemiology
Health Department
1730 East Elm Street
PO Box 570
Jefferson City, MO 65102

(314) 751-6411

Radon   Bureau of Radiological Health
                                   Missouri Department of Health
                                                   1730 E. Elm
                                                   PO Box 570
                                        Jefferson City, MO 65102
                                              (800) 669-7236
                                              (314) 751-6083

Water   Public Drinking Water Program
                        Missouri Department of Natural Resources
                                                   PO Box 176
                                        Jefferson City, MO 65102
                                              (314) 751-3241

Montana:

Asbestos   Health and Environmental Science
                                             Cogswell Building
                                             Helena, MT 59620
                                              (406) 444-3948

Radon   Occupational Health Bureau
          Montana Department of Health and Environmental Sciences
                                        Cogswell Building A113
                                             Helena, MT 59620
                                              (406) 444-3671

Water   Drinking Water Section
                                            Water Quality Bureau
                              Health and Environmental Services
                                                  Room A206
                                             Cogswell Building
                                             Helena, MT 59620

Nebraska:

Asbestos   Asbestos Program Coordinator
                                   Nebraska Department of Health
                                      301 Centennial Mall South
                                                 PO Box 95007
                                             Lincoln, NE 68509
                                              (402) 471-2541

Radon   Division of Radiological Health
                                   Nebraska Department of Health
                                      301 Centennial Mall South
                                                 PO Box 95007
                                             Lincoln, NE 68509

(402) 471-2168

Water   Division of Environmental Health and Housing
Nebraska Department of Health
PO Box 95007
Lincoln, NE 68509
(402) 471-2541

Nevada:

Radon   Radiological Health Section
Health Division
Nevada Department of Human Resources
505 East King Street
Carson City, NV 89710
(702) 885-5394

Water   Public Health Engineering
Nevada Department of Human Resources
Room 103
505 East King Street
Carson City, NV 89710
(702) 885-4750

New Hampshire:

Radon   Bureau of Radiological Health
Division of Public Health Services
Health and Welfare Building
6 Hazen Drive
Concord, NH 03301-6527
(603) 271-4674

Water   Water Supply Division
Water Supply and Pollution Control
Commission
PO Box 95
Hazen Drive
Concord, NH 03301
(603) 271-3503

New Jersey:

Asbestos   New Jersey Department of Health
Asbestos Control Service
CN 360
Trenton, NJ 08625
(609) 984-2193

Radon   Radiation Protection Element
         New Jersey Department of Environmental Protection
                                   729 Alexander Road
                                   Princeton, NJ 08540
                                       (800) 648-0394
                                       (609) 987-6402

Water   Bureau of Potable Water
                                   Division of Water Resources
         New Jersey Department of Environmental Protection
                                       PO Box CN-029
                                       Trenton, NJ 06825
                                       (609) 984-7945

New Mexico:

Radon   Radiation Licensing and Registration Section
         New Mexico Environmental Improvement Division
                                   1190 St. Francis Drive
                                   Santa Fe, NM 87504-0968
                                       (505) 827-2773

Water   Health Program Manager
                                       Water Supply Section
                          Environmental Improvement Division
                                          PO Box 968
                                   Santa Fe, NM 87504-0968
                                       (505) 827-2778

New York:

Radon   Bureau of Environmental Radiation Protection
                          New York State Health Department
                                   2 University Plaza
                                   Albany, NY 12237
                                       (800) 458-1158
                                       (518) 458-6450

Water   Bureau of Public Water Supply Protection
                          New York State Department of Health
                                   Office of Public Health
                                          Room 478
                                   Corning Tower Building
                                   Albany, NY 12237
                                       (518) 474-5577

North Carolina:

Asbestos   North Carolina Division of Health Services
                                   Cooper Memorial Building

Room 3011
PO Box 2091
225 North McDowell Street
Raliegh, NC 27602
(919) 733-0820

Radon

Radiation Protection Section
Division of Facility Services
North Carolina Department of Human Resources
701 Barbour Drive
Raliegh, NC 27603-2008
(919) 733-4283

Water

Water Supply Branch
Division of Public Health Services
Department of Human Resources
Bath Building
PO Box 2091
Raliegh, NC 27602-2091
(919) 733-2321

North Dakota:

Asbestos

North Dakota Department of Health
Missouri Office Building
PO Box 5520
Bismarck, ND 58502
(701) 224-2348

Radon

North Dakota Department of Health
Missouri Office Building
1200 Missouri Avenue
Room 304
PO Box 5520
Bismarck, ND 58502-5520
(701) 224-2348

Water

Division of Water Supply and Pollution Control
State Department of Health
1200 Missouri Avenue
Bismarck, ND 58501
(701) 224-2370

Ohio:

Asbestos

Ohio Department of Health
246 North High Street
PO Box 118
Columbus, OH 43266-0118
(614) 466-1450

Radon   Radiological Health Program
                               Ohio Department of Health
                               1224 Kinnear Road
                               Suite 120
                               Columbus, OH 43212
                               (800) 523-4439
                               (614) 644-2727

Water   Office of Public Water Supply
                               Ohio Environmental Protection Agency
                               361 East Broad Street
                               PO Box 1049
                               Colombus, OH 43216
                               (614) 466-8307

Oklahoma:

Asbestos & Radon Radiation and Special Hazards Service
                               Oklahoma State Department of Health
                               PO Box 53551
                               Oklahoma City, OK 73152
                               (405) 271-5221

Water   Water Facility Engineering Service
                               Oklahoma State Department of Health
                               PO Box 53551
                               Oklahoma City, OK 73152
                               (405) 271-5204

Oregon:

Radon   Oregon State Health Department
                               1400 SW 5th Avenue
                               Portland, OR 97201
                               (503) 229-5797

Water   Drinking Water Systems Section
                               Department of Human Resources
                               Health Division
                               1400 SW 5th Avenue
                               Portland, OR 97201
                               (503) 229-6310

Pennsylvania:

Radon   Department of Environmental Resources
                               Bureau of Radiation Protection
                               PO Box 2063
                               Harrisburg, PA 17120

(800) 23-RADON
(717) 787-2480

Water

Bureau of Water Supply
Department of Environmental Resources
PO Box 2063
Harrisburg, PA 17120
(717) 787-9035

Puerto Rico:

Asbestos

Puerto Rico Environmental Quality Board
204 Pumarada Street
10th Floor
PO Box 11488
San Turce, PR 00910
(809) 722-0077

Radon

Puerto Rico Radiological Health Division
GPO Call Box 70184
Rio Piedras, PR 00936
(809) 767-3563

Water

Drinking Water Supply Supervision Program
Puerto Rico Department of Health
PO Box 70184
San Juan, PR 00936
(809) 766-1616

Rhode Island:

Asbestos &
Radon

Occupational Health and Radiation
Rhode Island Department of Health
206 Cannon Building
75 Davis Street
Providence, RI 02908
(401) 277-2438 (radon) 277-3601 (asbestos)

Water

Division of Water Supply
Rhode Island Department of Health
75 Davis Street
Health Building
Providence, RI 02908
(401) 277-6867

South Carolina:

Radon

Bureau of Radiological Health

South Carolina Department of Health and Environmental
Control

2600 Bull Street
Columbia, SC 29201
(803) 734-4700 ext. 4631

Water   Division of Water Supply
Department of Health and Environmental Control
2600 Bull Street
Columbia, SC 29201
(803) 734-5310

South Dakota:

Radon   Division of Air Quality and Solid Waste
South Dakota Department of Water and Natural Resources
Joe Foss Building
Room 217
523 East Capital
Pierre, SD 57501-3181
(605) 773-3153

Water   Bureau of Drinking Water
Department of Water and Natural Resources
Joe Foss Building
523 Capital Avenue, East
Pierre, SD 57501
(605) 773-3151

Tennessee:

Radon   Division of Air Pollution Control
Bureau of Environmental Health
Department of Health and Environment
Custom House
701 Broadway
Nashville, TN 37219-5403
(615) 741-4634

Water   Division of Water Supply
Bureau of Environment
Tennessee Department of Health and Environment
150 Ninth Avenue, North
Nashville, TN 37219-5405
(615) 741-6636

Texas:

Asbestos   Occupational Health Program
1100 West 49th Street

Austin, TX 78756
(512) 458-7254

Radon   Bureau of Radiation Control
                         Texas Department of Health
                         1100 West 49th Street
                         Austin, TX 78756-3189
                         (512) 835-7000

Water   Division of Water Hygiene
                         Texas Department of Health
                         1100 West 49th Street
                         Austin, TX 78756
                         (512) 458-7533

Utah:

Asbestos & Radon   Department of Health
                              288 North, 1460 West
                              PO Box 16690
                         Salt Lake City, UT 84116-0690
              (801) 538-6734 (radon) (801) 538-6121 (asbestos)

Water   Bureau of Public Water Supplies
                         Utah Department of Health
                         Room 2007
                         288 North 1460 West
                         Salt Lake City, UT 84111
                         (801) 538-6159

Vermont:

Asbestos   Vermont Department of Health
                         Asbestos Program
                         60 Main Street
                         PO Box 70
                         Burlington, VT 05402
                         (802) 863-7231

Radon   Division of Occupational and Radiological Health
                         Vermont Department of Health
                         10 Baldwin Street
                         Montpelier, VT 05602
                         (802) 828-2886

Water   Sanitary Engineering
                         Division of Environmental Health
                         Vermont Department of Health
                         60 Main Street

PO Box 70
Burlington, VT 05401
(802) 863-7220

Virginia:

Radon

Bureau of Radiological Health
Department of Health
109 Governor Street
Richmond, VA 23219
(800) 468-0138
(804) 786-5932

Water

Bureau of Water Supply Engineering
Virginia Department of Health
James Madison Building
109 Governor Street
Richmond, VA 23219
(804) 786-1766

Virgin Islands:

Asbestos &
Radon

Planning and Natural Resources
Division of Environmental Protection
179 Altona and Welgunst
Charlotte Amelia
St. Thomas, V.I. 00802
(809) 774-3411

Washington:

Radon

Environmental Protection Section
Washington Office of Radiation Protection
Thurston AirDustrial Center
Building 5
Mail Stop LE-13
Olympia, WA 98504
(800) 323-9727
(206) 586-3303

Water

Drinking Water Operations
Mail Stop LD-11
Olympia, Washington 98504
(206) 753-5954

West Virginia:

Radon

Industrial Hygiene Division
West Virginia Department of Health
151 11th Avenue

South Charleston, WV 25303
(304) 348-3526/3427

Water

Drinking Water Division
Office of Environmental Health Services
Department of Health
1800 Washington Street, East
Charleston, WV 25305
(304) 348-2981

Wisconsin:

Asbestos

Wisconsin Division of Health
PO Box 309
Madison, WI 53701
(608) 266-9337

Radon

Radiation Protection Section
Division of Health
Wisconsin Department of Health and Social Services
5708 Odana Road
Madison, WI 53719
(608) 273-5180

Water

Bureau of Water Supply
Department of Natural Resources
Box 7921
Madison, WI 53707
(608) 267-7651

Wyoming:

Radon

Radiological Health Services
Wyoming Department of Health and Social Services
Hathway Building
Fourth Floor
Cheyenne, WY 82002-0710
(307) 777-6015

Water

Water Quality Division
Wyoming Department of Environmental Quality
401 West 19th Street
Cheyenne, WY 82002
(307) 777-7781

Index